THE WEBINAR WAY

The Single Most Effective Way to Promote Your Services, Drive Leads AND Sell a Ton of Products!

SHERRIE ROSE

In Praise of Webinars

"The last two webinars I've run have generated over $3.8 Million dollars in gross revenue. Webinars have truly changed my life and how I go about running my business and consulting with my clients. I now look for ways to include a webinar in every promotion or launch."

– Fernando Cruz

"I was so tired of seeing annoying sales letters that took all afternoon to read and that were largely filled with hype… when I discovered webinars I knew that it was a game changer. Webinars allowed me to convey my message and tell my story in a passionate, authentic and engaging manner… oh, and best of all, my sales rocketed. **If I could only have one business tool, it would be webinars."**

– Dean Hunt, DeanHunt.com

"If it weren't for webinars you wouldn't be reading this quote. My first webinar netted over $13K – I have gone on to do millions using webinars. I love webinars!"

– Sean Malarkey, Co-Founder, Magnetic Webinars

"Webinars took me to the next level in my business. The conversion rates were 10X higher than anything else we have done. You would be CRAZY if you don't start using them!"

– Joel Peterson, AutoWebinarPlayer.com

"Webinars are second only to face-to-face selling for making sales for our businesses and, unless you have an unlimited army of

salespeople, a webinar really is second to none!"

– Dr. Mike Woo-Ming

"One webinar brought in $106,000.00 in sales … as a TEST! Using automated webinars, I've been getting a 300% ROI on my marketing."

– Frank Kern

"When done right, webinars are an incredible tool to connect with your customers, provide more value, and make more sales. Anyone who has a high-value product or service for sale should learn how to incorporate webinars into their sales process."

– Wil Mattos, RapidCrush.com

"Webinars help you to reach your outcome faster. Webinars add interaction to your online content because great content means nothing if no one remembers or uses it. Webinars increase interaction and engagement with your audience so they remember what you said AND use it."

– Jeremie Miller

"Webinars are the new infomercial for entrepreneurs."

– Bart Christian, Southwest Training Systems

"Webinars are one of the most recession-proof marketing strategies you can use today."

– John C. Robinson, PassionQuest Technologies

"Webinars are a profit-pulling, time-saving, cost-reducing, relationship-building magnet…and if you're not using them, you are either rich or do not know what they are!"

– Tim Bennett, Argonette.com

"1.5 million in sales on automated webinars."

– Amish Shah

"Over the past 5 years, I've used webinars to train salespeople, educate prospects, motivate teams, promote products and even help raise capital. I believe webinars should be a part of every company's communication and sales arsenal."

– Gary Gil

"I have done 2,000 webinars over the past 6+ years, and some have done as much as $23,000+ in revenue in a single webinar broadcast."

– Ernie De Los Santos

"Last year we did over $1.8 million dollars using Live and Automated Webinars… basically if you're not using them in your business, then you're missing the boat!"

– Dax Aurand, KGB media group

When my Webinar day arrived, I was so nervous… I found my groove and delivered some quality content. At the end of my presentation, I threw up my personal PayPal link and offered a $150 Advanced LinkedIn Bootcamp… When I checked out my inbox, I almost cried… My inbox was full of messages, and they all said the same thing: "You've received a payment from…" I logged into my PayPal account and saw $6,200 sitting in it!

I had finally figured out how to make real money!

– Chris Ducker, best-selling author of
Rise of the Youpreneur:
The Definitive Guide to Becoming the Go-To Leader in Your Industry and Building a Future-Proof Business

 Publisher Omtiva.

ISBN : 978-0-999-37470-2
MHID : 0-999-37470-2

e-ISBN : 978-0-9993747-1-9
e-MHID : 0-9993747-1-9

For information contact:

http://www.TheWebinarWay.com

The Webinar Way – 2nd edition

First edition published October 2012

Subjects: LCSH: Business Presentations. | Sales Presentations. | BISAC: BUSINESS & ECONOMICS/ Business Communication / Meetings & Presentations | BUSINESS & ECONOMICS/ Skills

Julia,

May you succeed the Webinar Way!

Sherrie

Dec 2018

THE WEBINAR WAY

SHERRIE ROSE

TABLE OF CONTENTS

A Note to You, Our Reader xi

FOREWORD by Mari Smith xiii

Preface to the Second Edition xiv

Acknowledgements xv

PART I WEBINAR QUICK START 1

Webinar Quick Start 2

What is a Webinar? 3

WAMO Method 6

The Five UPs 13

3C by 3T Matrix for Webinars 14

7 Basics for Success in Webinars 18

PART II PAYDAY WEBINARS 21

Why You Must Track Your Webinar Metrics 22

Examples of Successful Webinar Metrics 24

The Webinar Way Profit Calculator 26

Why Webinars Are Your Next Payday 28

Three Big Whys of Webinars 30

PART III 7 PILLARS OF THE WEBINAR WAY 31

7 Pillars of the Webinar Way 32

Pillar 1: PERSPECTIVE 35

Pillar 2: PLAN 53

Pillar 3: PROMOTE 71

Pillar 4: PRESENT 103

Pillar 5: POWER POSITION 143

Pillar 6: PITCH 161

Pillar 7: PARTNER 191

PART IV THE WEBINAR LIFESTYLE 211

The Webinar Lifestyle 212

Perpetual Profits – Automated Webinars 215

Claim Your Webinar Strategy Session
& Start Your Own Perpetual Profit System 222

PART V The Webinar Way Resources 227

The Webinar Way RESOURCES 228

Hot Training: THE POWER OF WEBINARS 230

ABOUT SHERRIE ROSE 232

ABOUT THE WEBINAR WAY 233

POWER OF WEBINARS 234

FREE GIFT 235

A Note to You, Our Reader

As webinar masters, trainers, coaches and product developers, we have experienced many people around the world at live events, online, and through social media. Stories and examples in this book reflect experiences, interactions or syntheses with friends, members of the same social circles, clients and associates. Relevant details are highlighted and other details may be left out because they are not pertinent to the main teaching point. And, in full disclosure, as examples, some of the data and information has been pulled directly from public websites and included in various sections of the book.

The bonuses and tools mentioned throughout this book are available by registering on *The Webinar Way* website. See the section About *The Webinar Way* at the back of this book for links to the Facebook Page and Group, Google+ Community, and Pinterest for images and examples. As an owner of *The Webinar Way*, you are eligible to claim a Webinar Strategy Session to brainstorm, review, and expand your webinar success.

If you are here "looking inside" the Kindle edition and do not have a Kindle Device to get to the juicy details, you can get a free Kindle Reader that works on your computer and lets you read books instantly.

All software, webinar platforms, companies and other entities mentioned in this book most likely have intellectual properties with all rights and privileges conferred. Any comments and opinions are those of the authors and are true as of this writing, but may not be true as systems, software and opinions may change going forward.

Also, whatever titles we use are to create distinction. Sherrie calls herself *The Relationship Investor*. We are not medical doctors, licensed psychologists, psychiatrists, neuroscientists, lawyers, and legal or financial strategists. We are sharing this information from what we've learned online over the years, and none of the information is intended, or should be construed, to be professional medical, financial, or legal advice. If you need help in those areas, consult area-specific certified professionals.

Every effort has been made to accurately represent the techniques and strategies in this book. There is no guarantee that you will earn any money using the techniques and ideas presented. Examples in the book are not to be interpreted as a promise or guarantee of earnings. Earnings potential is entirely dependent on the person using the ideas and techniques. We do not purport webinars as a "get rich scheme." The complementary interviews on *The Webinar Way* website represent the ideas, successes, and techniques of each specific person.

Your level of success in attaining any results from the information provided in this book depends on the time you devote, ideas and techniques implemented, and various skills. Since these factors differ according to individuals, we cannot guarantee your success or income level, nor are we responsible for any of your actions. Many factors will be important in determining your actual results and no guarantees are made that you will achieve results similar to anybody else's. We are not responsible for what happens in your life or your finances including anything bad or good that happens as a result of following the information mentioned in this book.

With that said, have fun and be ready to engage in your first pilot webinar, or your 1000th webinar!

Sherrie Rose

FOREWORD BY MARI SMITH

I am here to share with you that webinars are a phenomenal tool to have in your marketing toolkit.

I also say that there is no amount of sophisticated technology that can take the place of one-on-one connecting in person: shaking hands, making eye contact, pressing the flesh, seeing body language. But, guess what? The next best thing is WEBINARS!

Live webinars are the next best thing to in-person contact. I offer free webinars. I look for timely topics. I just led a live streaming webinar with 5,700 people who participated (10,000 registered) from all over the world connected up on the webinar. It was phenomenal! Then I recorded the webinar so the replay can be played back. It gives you more material for mp3 audio and it can also be transcribed. Webinars are a fantastic marketing tool!

When you have live people tuning in, make an offer—an irresistible offer—and send them to a link. Give them the link and maybe a discount code for the offer if they sign-up by a certain time. Make it really obvious.

Webinars and live stream webinars that are TV quality and more casual work very well; don't set yourself up to be so perfect. Just start somewhere with your webinar and gather an audience who will participate with you!

It's *The Webinar Way*!

Mari Smith

Facebook Expert, Social Media Thought Leader Extraordinaire

See Mari on a webinar:

www.TheWebinarWay.com/MariSmith

PREFACE TO THE SECOND EDITION

It has been over five years since the first edition of this book presented readers with the *7 Pillars of The Webinar Way.* Webinars have gone from a mysterious wonder to a commonplace business tool. This edition (1) provides technical corrections, updates, and clarifications of the original book, and (2) adds summaries of new developments in software platforms available in the marketplace.

The main audience remains entrepreneurs, coaches, consultants and those people who want to profit by employing webinars in their business.

Acknowledgements

There are many wonderful people who contributed to this book in various forms. Each outstanding person is acknowledged on several unique web pages:

http://bookacknowledgements.com/thewebinarway/

## PART I

WEBINAR QUICK START

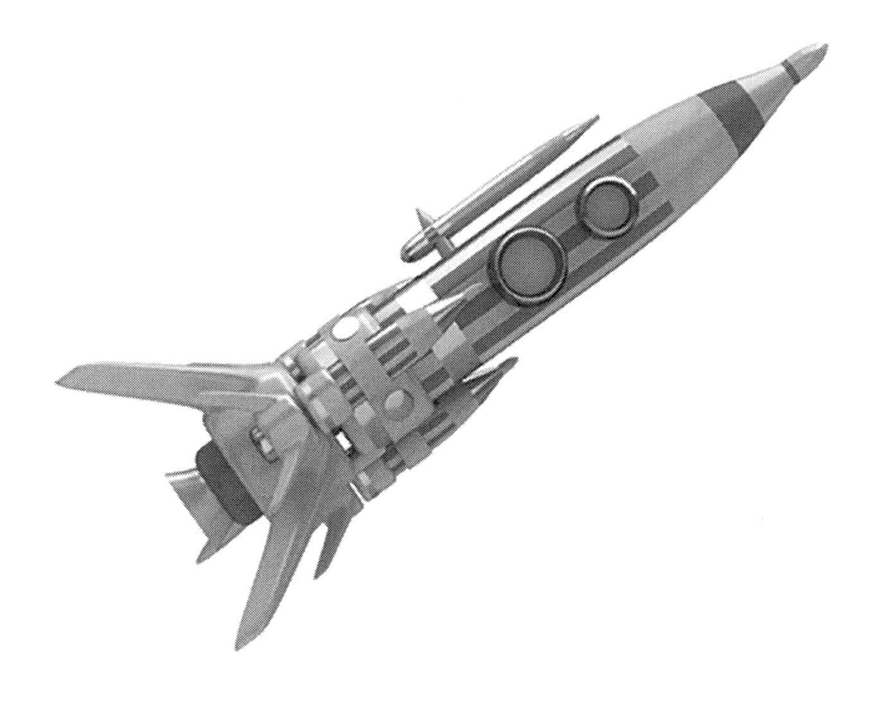

WEBINAR QUICK START

There is a shift happening in the marketplace between how products and services are received by prospective customers because the Internet provides instant access to people and information. As a result, many entrepreneurs and businesses are being left in the digital dust because they are not showing up, "live and in-person," to educate, engage, entertain and enrich their customers. This is where webinars come in.

In this introductory book, you will discover the WAMO Approach to webinars, the 3C by 3T matrix, and *The 7 Pillars of The Webinar Way*, as well as get a glimpse into the ultimate *Webinar Lifestyle.*

> **This book helps entrepreneurs, business professionals, coaches and organizations understand HOW to harness**
> **THE POWER OF WEBINARS**
> **to reach your desired goals so that you enjoy loyal customers, raving fans, authority status resulting in big profits and a better lifestyle!**
> **Because that's *The Webinar Way!***

Most of the links in this book are web pages on the website www.TheWebinarWay.com and, because things change quickly online, we did not want to give a direct link. The links are active at the time this book is being published, but they may not be valid forever.

WHAT IS A WEBINAR?

"Webinars work. They provide the benefits of in-person seminars without the costs, hassle, and limitations that come with live in-person events."

The term webinar is a combination of the words **web** and **seminar**. At one point someone trademarked the word but now it is in the public domain.

A webinar is a seminar done over the internet. Its predecessor, the teleseminar, provided only audio, webinars offer both audio and visuals, usually in the form of a slide deck.

The concept of a webinar has been described as a web conference, webcast, Internet meeting, online conference, web meeting, and electronic meeting, to name a few.

Webinar means you have incorporated a visual element.

The term webinar refers to an online presentation and can be any combination of slides and audio, video webcast with screen displays, slides and streaming video, etc.

A webinar can become YOUR PRODUCT, if you charge a fee. A webinar can be used as a lead generation tool. A webinar can promote a product or service. A webinar can be a promotions vehicle. Many marketing funnels include one or more webinars.

Chad Kerby, representing Infusionsoft, a popular customer relationship management system, recommends webinars as step one (seven steps in a marketing funnel process) by attracting traffic with great content.

Stephen Renton, author and one of the experts interviewed for *The Webinar Way*, concisely describes a webinar as **"an interactive audio-visual presentation which is broadcast over the Internet, to demonstrate a product, service, or to provide training to a group of participants. You can have one or more presenters and there can be up to 1,000 participants on a single webinar."**

A webinar is an interactive, audiovisual, online broadcast. Thousands of participants can watch and actively participate in a webinar, live as well as on-demand, for anytime consumption. Some webinar platforms, like Online Seminar, are completely web-based, and accessible from any device, smartphone, and laptop, with no software or installation required. After a simple registration process, your target audience can watch the webinar from any location.

Webinars are used by individual entrepreneurs, joint venture partners, collaborative teams, corporations, and non-profit organizations.

Why Webinars Benefit You

Webinars are one of the best tools for individuals and companies for a reason—they give you the ability to customize your message and make it truly one of a kind! Whether you're new to online business or you want a new income stream, here are a few reasons to add a webinar presentation into your marketing mix to creating awareness and customer loyalty:

- You have an important message to get out to the world.
- You want an easy way to reach your audience.
- You want to get paid to teach and **educate**.
- You want to profit from your expertise and be seen as **THE Authority** in your market.

- You want a high-level of interaction experience with your fans, prospects and customers.
- You want to reduce or eliminate the time and expense of speaking seminars (airfare, venue rental, equipment costs, other fees, etc.).
- You want the ability to **automate your income**.
- You want to benefit from a 24/7 system to generate continuous prospects who convert easily into customers.

Most importantly, you want all of the benefits giving you financial profits and freedom of choice that come when you live *The Webinar Lifestyle.*

WAMO METHOD

> ***"If you have an important point to make, don't try to be subtle or clever. Use a pile driver. Hit the point once. Then come back and hit it again. Then hit it a third time – a tremendous whack."***
>
> *- Sir Winston Churchill*

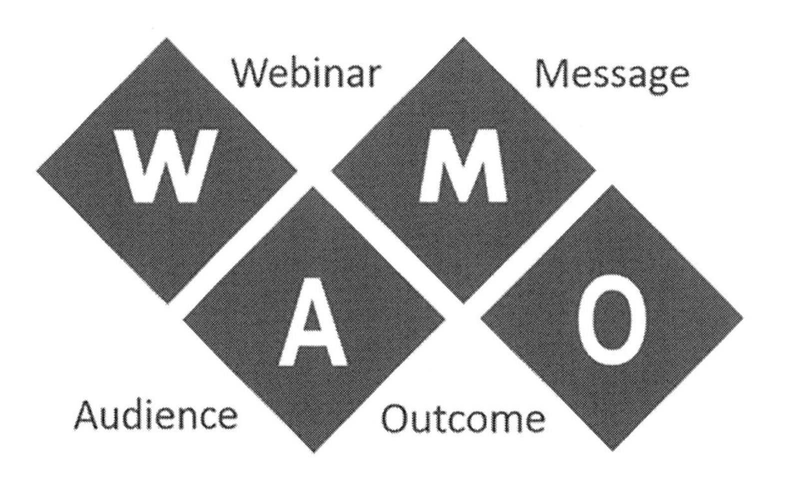

There are so many elements to consider in running a webinar event, just like running a live event. If you present on stage then you must understand that a new medium demands a different approach, and you must adapt to the new environment. A definitive blueprint or formula for webinars does not really exist, but there are some basic elements to consider.

Our WAMO Method or Approach involves four basic elements. The first is to determine your objective, then craft a powerful webinar presentation around your message, designed to satisfy your desired outcome while entertaining, educating, and enriching your audience. The WAMO Approach gives you an overview to get started on webinars.

Ed Dale, who has conducted many successful webinars, loved hearing about the WAMO Approach to webinars. You can learn more about it in his interview, as it is discussed in detail. All *The Webinar Way* interviews are listed in the Resource Section of this book.

WAMO is an acronym for Webinar, Audience, Message and Outcome.

- **Webinar** – The '*What* and *Why*.' What is it about and why should I care? What are the problems that your potential webinar participant is facing? The webinar is a promotion vehicle, selling mechanism, as well as a training medium and possible product. You can take a simmering issue and make it boil so it becomes urgent.
- **Audience** – Attracting your audience with webinars. Turning your attendees into participants, learners, repeat customers and RAVING FANS! We really prefer to call the audience 'participants' but that did not work with the acronym!
- **Message** – Your message, marketing and model. Design and deliver an experience that highlights your message.
- **Outcome** – Start with your desired outcome, your objective, your offer, your action point. The outcome theme runs through promotional messages to attract your audience and, ultimately, your actual webinar outcome. A successful webinar is one that achieves your outcome.

You really want to use the acronym backwards starting with O: Outcome. You've heard many wise sages state that you must know your destination, your outcome. Ask yourself,

"Would you get in a taxicab and let the driver take you wherever he wants?" You must have a destination plan, which is your desired outcome.

Start with your intention, your purpose. Purpose defines "what's in it for me" (WIIFM) for the audience. This is the message that comes through with your webinar title, promotional headlines, and supporting copy and images. To make your webinar more relevant, you can tie it to a current trend. Your headline, your registration page, and your promise as you begin the webinar, and the actual webinar content that you deliver, must be consistent.

If your outcome is to convert your webinar participant into a paying customer, there are several factors that affect the attendee's decision to click the buy button and take action in front of their computer monitor, without meeting you in person. Be clear on your audience's needs, especially if you plan on creating a webinar series. Ideally, you target the same market that your business already knows and markets in other ways, so webinars are part of your overall marketing mix. Attracting the right target audience, having an intriguing title and surrounding promotional copy, turning the audience into participants and delivering on your promises with the right message to market match is critical. You reach your audience through all the right messages on a relevant email list, registration page or another form of media, get their attention, build their interest, channel their desire and give a call to action that they will act on, now!

Webinars contain the message in addition to acting as the medium for delivery. This includes the visual messages, with photos and graphics, videos and possibly online demonstrations. Consistency helps with orientation so a webinar attendee knows they are on the right webinar and they'll get their questions answered. Create a similar style so there is congruency, but not so similar that it seems boring.

The WAMO Method is an overview approach to get you started. We will discuss your message in more detail regarding promotion and presentation in *The 7 Pillars of The Webinar Way* to success in Part III of this book.

If the webinar is the medium, your message must make sense to your audience with a message-to-market match. There are positioning or awareness webinars, educational webinars, sampling or demonstration webinars, sales conversion webinars and post-sale webinars to name a few.

Let's look at four popular webinars (there are various types) and their desired outcomes:

1. Educational Webinar Format

The outcome is to grow your audience by providing primarily educational content. This attracts a lot of people by providing value, and letting them know there is "no sales pitch." However, you still must ask for some interaction, such as sending tweets or Facebook comments or other social media activity before, during, and after the webinar. This type of webinar is good for branding, helping you build your celebrity and authority and putting you in the Power Position.

2. Coach/Consultant Format

The outcome is to identify prospective clients by offering a free strategy call after the webinar. This weeds out the visitors from those people truly interested in your main offer. You'll need calendar software to schedule the calls and you'll provide the details on the webinar. These free calls (under many names such as strategy, consultation, triage, discovery, etc.) have no financial risk and the cost is time. This puts you in the Power Position as the one who provides answers even if the prospective client does not purchase your coaching program or consultation package.

3. Demonstration Webinar Format

The outcome is two-fold: grow your audience and sell your product or service. A webinar is the perfect medium for a software demonstration. The conversion rate on webinars where you're demonstrating software or web-based tools is extremely high. Often 10-20% of the people that register for demonstration webinars will actually end up buying. You can also enlist beta-testers to test your software with a pre-release version. These, ideally, will turn into testimonials for you.

4. Free Training with Sales Conversion Webinar Format

The outcome is two-fold: grow your audience and sell your product or service. You provide stellar content and training that is so compelling that the webinar participants want more, and you offer a product or service in a "sales pitch" with an opportunity to purchase. The opportunity may include paying for additional in-depth training via webinars.

Webinars can also be planned as a series. Once you have an active audience who has grown to trust you, you can survey your webinar participants for another hot topic for a future training webinar. With a webinar series, you can leverage a library of webinar recordings in a membership site or repurpose the content. Your topic or theme may be of interest to a company that would like to sponsor the series. A webinar series is like putting on multiple events, so be prepared to do some work and handle it like event or project management.

If you want something simpler than a series, consider doing your webinar in segments. The first segment, webinar one, is pure content. The second webinar segment is for your product sales tour and special offers. If you are offering a strategy session or free consultation, you do not need two segments.

Webinars showing software demos are popular at Hubspot. Hubspot sells a software solution and uses that very software to attract its customers at a very low cost. Webinars are a big part of the marketing, sales and training process at Hubspot.

Hubspot has thousands of people sign up for their webinars. Mike Volpe of Hubspot says that people visit a website, read blog posts and download free eBooks—and these are all great lead generators. Reading a blog post may be a five minutes exercise, but, in the act of attending a webinar, you become a participant and give up to an hour of your time to focus on the subject of the webinar. Hubspot produces valuable content on their blog and attracts inbound traffic, which generates higher quality leads and conversions.

Hubspot earned the Guinness World Record for Webinars on a very broad educational topic webinar entitled "The Science of Social Media." This 2011 webinar drew upwards of 30,000 registrants and 10,000 people showed up, which is the current world record for the largest webinar ever.

Webinars are where the rubber meets the road, because you can engage and have conversations with your customers. Part of that conversation is the right message at the right time that starts before the webinar. Connection happens within that conversation.

Each action a prospect takes will bring them further along your marketing funnel. An interaction in the conversion pipeline may start with a lead generation promotion that gets your target to take an action such as signing up to get a free bonus or registering for a webinar.

A quick review of the three stages of your audience:

- A **Suspect** is everyone in your target audience
- A **Prospect** is anyone who has taken an action
- A **Customer/Client** is anyone who has purchased

There may be a few more interim stages before becoming a customer. The type of business or service you offer will determine the next stage. If you are selling a product, at the end of a webinar presentation your prospect can purchase and become a customer. If you are selling on behalf of a company or need to weed out the bad leads from the good leads, the next stage might be to fill out an application, to arrange for a consultation, or something of that nature to help self-select by choosing to act or to deselect by not acting. The person in the lead stage is providing you with more detailed information to help you to determine whether or not they are going to eventually become a customer. You can also consider creating an exclusive invitation where the prospect may apply to get approved to move to the next stage. Part of defining your outcome is determining what stages a prospect will go through to become your customer.

THE FIVE UPs

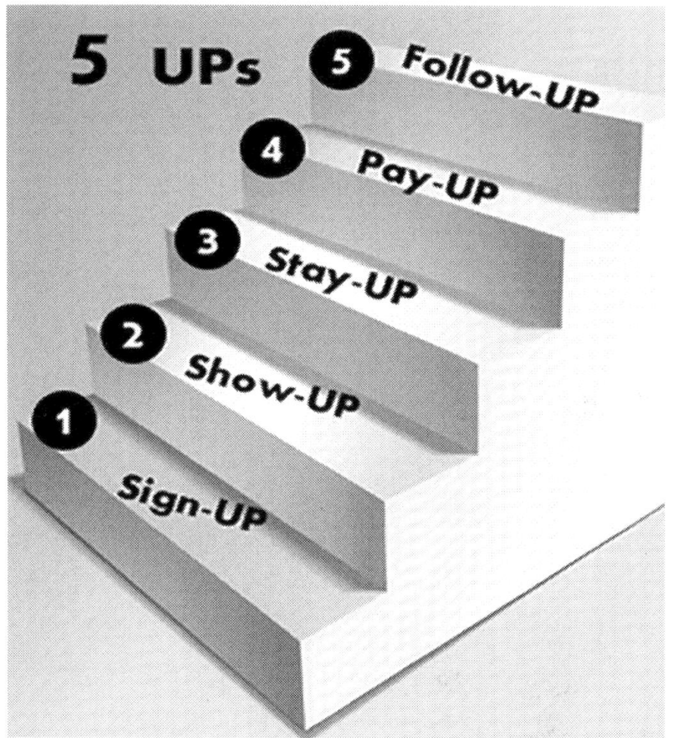

Figure 1

The Five Ups for Webinars

SIGN-UP: Get the Webinar Registration. Build your list of interested people.

SHOW-UP: Send reminders so attendees show up at the webinar event.

STAY-UP: Keep it exciting with Active Participants.

PAY-UP: During the pitch, Participants make a purchase or complete another Call to Action in the webinar close.

FOLLOW-UP: Use email, phone, social groups, and in-person to further the sale and build the relationship.

3C BY 3T MATRIX FOR WEBINARS

You now have clarity on your WAMO overview and your desired outcome is well defined. Here we go from broad to more focus. Now we'll look at the 3C Steps you should focus on.

The 3C by 3T Matrix gives you a high-level overview of the core of your webinar across time elements.

Consider the importance of your content. Before the webinar, you will be defining the title, presentation content, registration page content, follow-up emails' content, etc. These are all a part of your marketing funnel. To make a connection with your audience, you will have logistical steps, technical steps and, most important, you'll be concentrating on building rapport with your audience. Finally, you are not just conducting a webinar to generate leads and deliver exceptional content; your plan is to close and take your webinar participants to the next stage. That's your desired outcome.

The 3 Core Components (3C) to your webinar are Content, Connection and Close. Content, Connection and Close change with time as they move through the marketing funnel. We must add in the time components (3T): before, during and after the webinar. Before are your pre-webinar activities, during is your webinar event, and after are your post-webinar activities. How and what you share with your audience depends on the phase of before, during and after your webinar. Your target audience also changes as they experience the 3C by 3T webinar activities as they go from cold prospect to customer and hot raving fan!

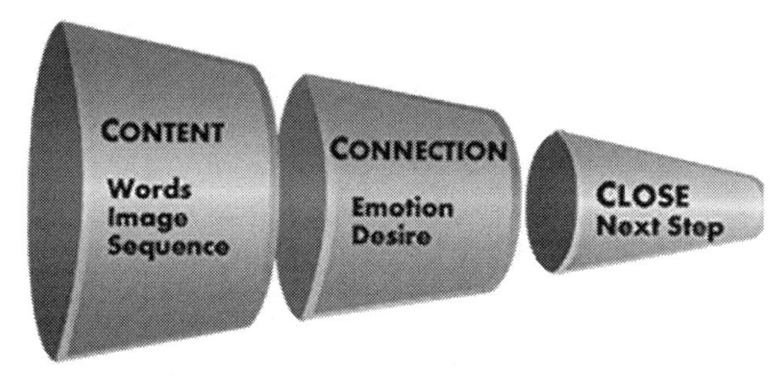

Figure 2

Think about the three core components as a funnel for each time period, before, during, and after the webinar.

3C x 3T MATRIX	CONTENT C1	CONNECTION C2	CLOSE C3
BEFORE T1 Pre-Webinar Activities *Suspects*	Promote to attract visitors, planning and preparation. Email sequence, campaign, web pages, videos, magnets, registration page. Create, curate, procure and practice presentation.	Begin conversation. How you appear in promotions. What can be found about you online that supports your message. Start to channel desire and evoke emotion.	Get webinar registration. Provide additional actions (share, follow, like social media). Take a survey. Warm up the audience for the live event.
DURING T2 WEBINAR EVENT *Prospects*	Presentation style & Prizes (bonuses, gifts). Activate emotion and senses. Turn passive webinar audience learners into active participants. **Entertain, Educate, Enrich.**	Control and guide conversation with Confidence, Pace, Tone of voice – Establish Power Position to creates instant celebrity and fame. Quality questions. **Engage.**	Clarity on the intended offer and steps leading up to the offer. Provide value. Ask for the action to be taken – Convert to sale or next step. **Execute.**
AFTER T3 Post-Webinar Activities *Customers & Fans*	Multiple tracks - Special web pages for Preferred (Paying) Customers and future customers and follow-up pages and emails. Optional: Notes, transcripts, slide deck.	Follow-up process – Stay top of mind, automated webinars. Join community (fan page, membership site). Deliver on your promise.	Follow-up email sequence, related offers, bonuses, upsells, webinar replay, encores, automated webinars.

Figure 3

Get a clear overview, get focused on the 3Cs, but don't get overwhelmed. Your messages need to have "must watch" content with excitement and sizzle to attract an audience. Your content will be attractive when it's important and informative to your target audience. There is a promise of what will be received on the webinar, such as specifics, case studies, steps, and, as Oren Klaff says, a "big idea" that answers a top question or solves a pressing problem.

A Persuasion Map can be used for storyboarding a webinar, a book, or a speech. Aristotle said, "*In making a speech one must study three points: first, the means of producing persuasion; second, the language; third the proper arrangement of the various parts of the speech.*" The same goes for a webinar.

Your big idea can be added to a Persuasion Map. Use the free Persuasion Map, which is one of the bonuses that you receive when you sign up on *The Webinar Way* website. Listen to Matt Gillogly's interview to hear how he creates his webinar content with the ideas behind the Persuasion Map.

Get the free Persuasion Map, which is one of the bonuses that you receive when you sign up on *The Webinar Way* website: http://TheWebinarWay.com.

A live webinar is an event and also has similar elements to a product launch. There are a lot of moving parts and there are usually other people playing parts or performing key roles. There are the pre-webinar activities, webinar "show" day and post-webinar activities. There are decisions to be made, logistics to coordinate and, fortunately, some of this can be setup on auto-pilot with proper planning.

The 3C by 3T Matrix gives you an idea of the timing of activities. Promotional activities before the webinar are key to success. Create a free giveaway, a "lead magnet" or "lead candy" that lets suspects opt-in on a web landing page. Distribute your promotions through various channels. Find out where they are and send your message. You need people to show up. What draws them in is your content. At each stage, connect and close them on the action you want them to execute. Automate the reminder sequences of emails. Plan webinar event companion materials, bonuses, and the post-webinar follow-up to nurture the leads you have generated. Advertising is recommended.

3T by 3C Matrix is also a reminder to take a tip from photographers and cinematographers, and to remember the "rule of thirds" for your slide images on your presentation. If you don't know what this is, check out the Resources section at the end of this book.

One of the most important things to do post-webinar is to review your performance. When your webinar concludes, you are not finished. It is recommended not to do a webinar on your own. Jump off the webinar and set up an immediate meeting with the other presenters, host, and moderators. Some platforms have private sub-conferences where you can get together to review and debrief. Debrief while it is still fresh to find the audience pulse and hot and cold points of your webinar.

You don't just record your webinar sessions for your audience. Record for yourself and be ready to revamp as needed. Review the recording and look for ways to improve your virtual delivery style, the smoothness of the webinar delivery, the cadence of presentation, slide and website transitions, and how you can increase interactivity on your next webinar.

Look at the survey results. You have tracked your visits, clicks, closing actions or sales. Go over your metrics with *The Webinar Way Profit Calculator,* which we will discuss in the Payday Webinars section of the book coming up next. Plan to debrief the host, presenters and other parties. Manage your evaluation process.

7 Basics for Success in Webinars (or Anything, for That Matter)

Now that you have your webinar started, let's take a quick look at the basics of success. The first four basics are about you. The last three basics are about other people. Webinars are a combination of you and other people, plus a little technology.

1. Trust yourself.
2. Break a few rules (not laws, just rules). Be unique, be different, become a maverick.
3. Don't be afraid to fail. *"Every adversity, every failure, every heartache carries with it the seed of an equal or greater benefit."* — Napoleon Hill
4. Work Hard, Work Right, Work Smart. You don't have to do it by yourself, but you do have to work. *"Hard work often leads to success. No work seldom does."* — Harvey Mackay
5. Provide value for your webinar participants. The value provided is a reflection of your job, your business, and community organizations. Give back and contribute.
6. The *Real Currency* is Relationship Riches. Aim to invest in yourself and invest and serve others. The return on investment is financial plus recurring emotional riches.
7. Ignore naysayers and uninformed critics. Find a coach or mentor who can guide you. Visit: WebinarCoach.com

Webinars use the connectivity of the Internet as the springboard to open a conversation with the right message, about an excellent product or service, to the right people, at the right time. The right conversation leads to conversions in sales or actions. It's *The Webinar Way*.

This page intentionally left blank

## PART II

PAYDAY WEBINARS

WHY YOU MUST TRACK YOUR WEBINAR METRICS

Done right, webinars are your next payday.

THE #1 most effective way to promote your services, drive leads, and sell a ton of products is a webinar. Webinars are the serious entrepreneur's favorite wealth builder.

Webinars are THE #1 way to present and educate your prospective customers and bring them to a buying decision so you and your customer both profit, because of the value they receive with your product or service.

Webinars are THE #1 way to wealth in the Internet arena. Many people who are involved in Internet marketing and social media employ webinars several times a week, and they attribute much of their wealth to webinars. There is serious wealth in webinars.

> **In the world of webinars, the ultimate currency is an experience that leads to additonal gains. You may benefit financially, but everyone benefits from the enriching experience. With webinars, you convert the conversation into currency.**

The most common "payday webinar" is comprised of an educational component (the content) and an offer (the close). The prospective customers (leads) are attracted by various promotions (connection), and if the registration page does its job (closes) then the lead is nurtured with additional communication until the webinar begins. The webinar presenter provides valuable content and creates a connection with the participants. At the end of the webinar, the offer (close) is indicated by providing a link to an outside order page to make a purchase.

Payday webinars are not the only kind of webinar. Some webinars are designed simply to inform, motivate or inspire. Payday webinars provide valuable educational content, as well as increase the influence of the webinar presenter who is seen as an authority in their field. Even if a webinar participant does not buy immediately, there is a payoff in growing your online influence.

Webinars are a conversation and are truly one of the best ways to create relationships with your participants. Webinars are a key tool in educating audiences and the webinar experience fosters a teacher-student relationship. Mari Smith, author several books including, *The New Relationship Marketing*, gives you **a ticket to attend her four-part webinar series as a FREE bonus for buying her book.** She records all sessions if you can't make them live, so you can go back and review them anytime. It is during Mari's webinars that you *bond with her* and then she offers you her paid training program. She also conducts livestream TV quality webinars for her audience.

The goal of a webinar is to create an enriching experience that leads to relationship riches: more fans, more customers, and more profits. That's *The Webinar Way*!

If you have visited the website *The Webinar Way* (www.TheWebinarWay.com) and you signed-up for your free bonuses, then you have probably listened to several interviews with top-notch entrepreneurs. They say thousands to millions of dollars of their income comes directly from webinars. Webinars can be your next big payday.

EXAMPLES OF SUCCESSFUL WEBINAR METRICS

Distribution List Size:	11,982
Total Clicks:	981
Percent of Clicks:	8.25%
Webinar Registrations:	981
Webinar Attendees:	246
Number of Sales:	15
Total Revenue (w/o upsell):	$44,955
Dollar Per Attendee:	$182.74

The next set of metrics are shared by Jason Drohn about his webinar.

- Webinar conversion: 47% on a $97 product (yes, that number is real and verified)
- Revenue Per Attendee: $41.29 (that is before upsells were added)
- Refund Rate: 0.3% – 30-day refund policy **(* That is Less Than 1% *)**

Lewis Howes on his first 30-minute webinar sold a $150 product to 40 people and made $6,300. Dave Foran, on his second webinar with about 80 people in attendance, converted at 24%. He took in over $14,000 in less than 90 minutes.

George Birnbach, a seasoned speaker, closed $120,000 worth of business on his first webinar.

Tristan's first webinar was a joint venture with no sales allowed. He worked with his coach, Taki Moore, to create a free content giveaway (an eBook, an audio recording, and a diagnostic audit/session). Tristan used the webinar to set up his giveaway offer, and sold on the strategy sessions. Based on that first webinar, he made $336,000 in sales.

The chapter on Pillar 7 of *The Webinar Way*, talks about partners. Joint Venture (JV) Partners are a major factor in webinar wealth. In the interview with Ty Cohen, you will hear him share his webinar secrets. Here are some of his webinar metrics with his JV partners. His is a $997 product mailed to the customer. EPC is earnings per click.

Ty's top four JV partners' gross sales (within 24 hours before emailing the webinar replay):

$122,456.42
$94,894.80
$59,887.40
$51,322.60
$49,142.85

Average Gross Revenue per webinar attendee: $201.12

Lowest Gross EPC: $6.00

Highest Gross EPC: $10.00

Average Webinar Registration Opt-In %: 58%

Highest Affiliate Webinar Registration Opt-In %: 77%

Lowest Affiliate Webinar Registration Opt-In %: 41%

Average Attendee Show Up %: 56%

Highest Attendee Show Up %: 65%

Lowest Attendee Show Up %: 51%

As you can see with these metrics, making sure you have an easy way to capture the right data and calculate your profits will be a valuable asset to you. Use *The Webinar Way Profit Calculator.*

THE WEBINAR WAY PROFIT CALCULATOR

We are providing all our readers, as our gift to you, The Webinar Way Profit Calculator. You will want this to calculate your webinar profits. Sign up on the website and the download link will be delivered via email along with other surprise bonuses.

Sign up on the website http://TheWebinarWay.com.

You may ask, "What is a good conversion rate for a webinar?" and the answer is "It depends." The factors such as target audience, content and price point play into conversion. Webinars with a price range of $400 to $1,000 can convert as high as 40% and much higher for participants registering for a free service, strategy session, or trial offer.

You've probably attended many webinars, but have you experienced doing them for yourself?

Experience gives you the confidence that webinars are the #1 way to sell and market your online business.

It may be a little intimidating or odd (talking to "yourself" while delivering your presentation). Your webinar is the best way to connect with your audience, all over the world, to share training, and of course, sell products because eventually it feels like you are having many one-on-one conversations.

With the right structure, you can confidently pitch six and seven-figure products and services for your business AND have your audience DEMAND that you sell them something.

With webinars, you can have a proven method of generating sales, growing your business and increasing your bottom-line profits. Creating an automated webinar that sells your product or service can save you time by eliminating the need to show up in-person at every time zone across the globe. We'll talk about Automated Webinars in Part IV. Your webinars can be set up to run automatically, week after week, month after month, and generating perpetual profits for your business.

"Profits are better than wages. Wages make you a living; profits make you a fortune." – Jim Rohn

If you aren't already using webinars, then you are missing an incredible opportunity for growth.

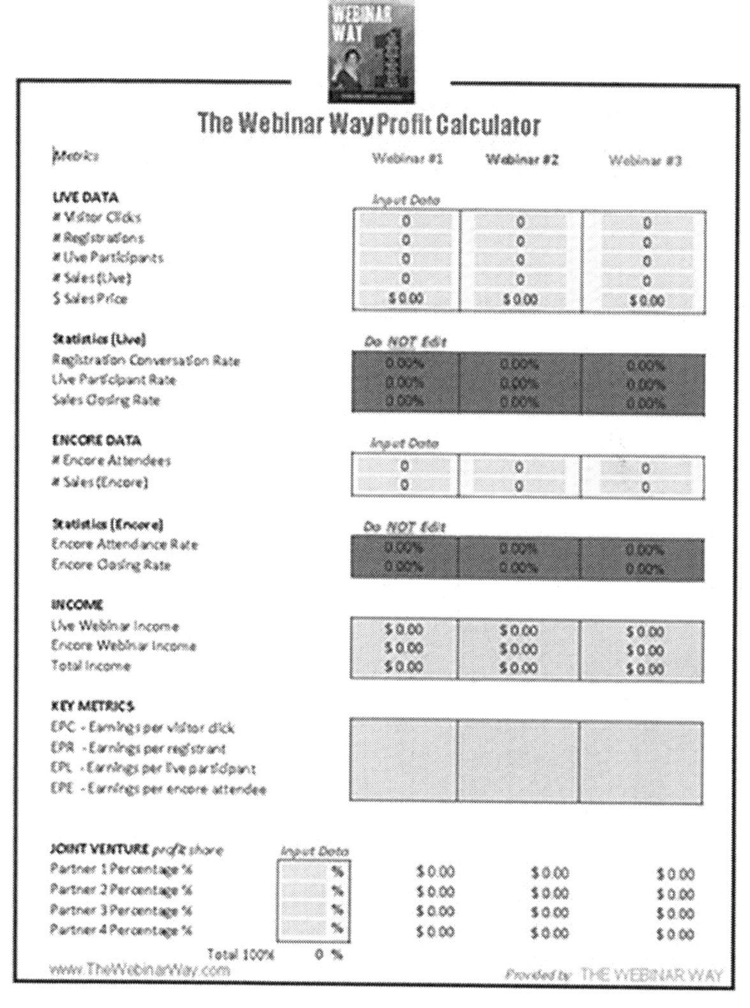

The Webinar Way Profit Calculator

Metrics	Webinar #1	Webinar #2	Webinar #3
LIVE DATA	*Input Data*		
# Visitor Clicks	0	0	0
# Registrations	0	0	0
# Live Participants	0	0	0
# Sales (Live)	0	0	0
$ Sales Price	$0.00	$0.00	$0.00
Statistics (Live)	*Do NOT Edit*		
Registration Conversation Rate	0.00%	0.00%	0.00%
Live Participant Rate	0.00%	0.00%	0.00%
Sales Closing Rate	0.00%	0.00%	0.00%
ENCORE DATA	*Input Data*		
# Encore Attendees	0	0	0
# Sales (Encore)	0	0	0
Statistics (Encore)	*Do NOT Edit*		
Encore Attendance Rate	0.00%	0.00%	0.00%
Encore Closing Rate	0.00%	0.00%	0.00%
INCOME			
Live Webinar Income	$0.00	$0.00	$0.00
Encore Webinar Income	$0.00	$0.00	$0.00
Total Income	$0.00	$0.00	$0.00
KEY METRICS			
EPC - Earnings per visitor click			
EPR - Earnings per registrant			
EPL - Earnings per live participant			
EPE - Earnings per encore attendee			

JOINT VENTURE *profit share*	*Input Data*			
Partner 1 Percentage %	%	$0.00	$0.00	$0.00
Partner 2 Percentage %	%	$0.00	$0.00	$0.00
Partner 3 Percentage %	%	$0.00	$0.00	$0.00
Partner 4 Percentage %	%	$0.00	$0.00	$0.00
Total 100%	0 %			

www.TheWebinarWay.com

Provided by THE WEBINAR WAY

Figure 4

Why Webinars Are Your Next Payday

Webinars can be used in virtually any industry. Webinars are a proven method for unlocking the sales potential for personality-driven brands, large and small businesses alike. If your customers can be found on the Internet or will go online to connect with you, then webinars can help dramatically grow your company's sales and profits.

The two simplest ways to make money with webinars are: a) charge people to attend, or b) provide free information and training, and convert that conversation into profit by closing with an offer that leads to a sale. The sale may be immediate or it may come after a second step after the webinar such as a phone call or meeting.

There are other ways to make money with webinars. A webinar is not a solo act. A webinar is an event combined with launch components, and it is the participants and the other "players" performing various roles in the webinar that can skyrocket your webinar into a wealth-creating machine.

If you are starting out, think of your webinar as a two-way conversation where you are actively engaging your customers and prospects to participate and find out exactly what they want. Then you can tailor your product and service to satisfy their needs. Your webinars may be completely free as you gather a following and begin to build your "tribe" and fan base.

You can even bundle the webinar recordings into a paid product, creating a new revenue source for you. For existing products, webinars can increase your sales conversions so you sell more.

If you are experienced, you'll want to fine-tune your presentation so the hot buttons to buy from you are crystal clear and irresistible. Remove all guesswork by testing and trying to figure out which webinar presentation sells the best. You'll also want to review your promotion and follow-up process and streamline it to optimize for conversions. As Peter Drucker has said, "You can't improve what you don't measure."

Webinars are a great way to leverage your time and, as the saying goes, time is money. It is a one-to-many method of selling but the experience is one-to-one. A webinar can work in conjunction with a sales team. Once your webinar is designed, optimized and proven to generate sales, each of your salespeople can use it as a template for their own sales presentations.

It goes without saying that you first have to have a product or service to sell. Then there are the components of the webinar:

- You must setup up the webinar software.
- You must script the webinar.
- You must prepare the slide deck.
- You must plan the email sequence.
- Other options: video, custom graphics and registration, page, upsells and downsells

Three Big Whys of Webinars

1. **Immersion**: Webinars are an incredibly immersive experience with interactivity, questions can be asked live and the content can be consumed. Make your presentation visually memorable and impactful.

2. **Real-time content sharing**: Using the webinar platform tools, easily share resources such as files or web links prepared into the delivery in advance or given out on the fly. This moves your participants down the funnel more quickly. During the replay recording those links are still active, which gives future webinar viewers the same access to the content that was delivered live.

3. **Cost-effective and Convenient**: Webinars are cost-effective and are less expensive than producing or attending a live event. Webinars offer a convenient way to deliver content presented by an expert. Webinars offer a much wider reach due to their virtual and global nature. There is no travel for participants and the content can be enjoyed from the convenience of the office or any location via mobile devices. The recorded replay webinar is available for immersion after the webinar, further increasing its cost-effectiveness and value. Webinar replay recordings are a convenient way of catching up on what may have been missed. The audience who watch a recorded on-demand webinar learn and gain value and continue to place more sales for the webinar creator.

## PART III

7 PILLARS OF THE WEBINAR WAY

7 Pillars of the Webinar Way

> ***"Over 80% of marketers rate webinars as one of their top 3 marketing tactics for lead generation."***
>
> *- Forrester Research*

There is "no one-size fits-all" solution for the perfect webinar. *The 7 Pillars of The Webinar Way* are principles that you can use no matter if the fashion or style of slide deck changes, or if the technology changes.

THE 7 PILLARS

Pillar 1: PERSPECTIVE

Passion, People, Purpose, Part

- **Passion:** What is it that you are teaching and sharing?
- **Purpose:** Where does the webinar fit in the overall scheme of your business?
- **People:** Who will benefit? Who are the other players?
- **Part:** What's your part? Which role(s) will you and other people perform?

Pillar 2: PLAN

Platform, Planning, Process, Priorities

- **Platform:** What do you look for in a webinar platform?
- **Planning:** Why does planning precede profit?
- **Process:** What do you include in your sales and marketing processes, campaigns, and funnels?
- **Priorities:** How do you determine your priorities in setting up and running a webinar?

Pillar 3: PROMOTE

Promotion, Pages, Proof, Pre-sell

- **Promotion:** What are the different ways to promote a webinar?
- **Pages:** What types of web pages are needed for the various aspects of a webinar?
- **Proof:** Why do testimonials and other forms of proof attract webinar registrations?
- **Pre-sell:** How do you pre-sell with benefits and creating "hooks?"

Pillar 4: PRESENT

Presentation, Presenters, Practice, Participants

- **Presentation:** What do you put in a high-converting webinar presentation?
- **Presenters:** How a webinar presenter can make or break the success of a webinar?
- **Practice:** Why does "practice make profit" with webinars?
- **Participants:** How do you turn a passive attendee into an active participant?

Pillar 5: POWER POSITION

Presence, Prize, Persuasion, Power Position

- **Presence:** How do you create a commanding presence to be seen as an authority?
- **Prize:** What are the different types of "prizing" as part of the webinar experience?

- **Persuasion:** What forms of persuasion turn participants into buyers and raving fans?
- **Power Position:** What is the Ultimate Power Position?

Pillar 6: PITCH

Profit Models, Promise, Pacing, Pitch Examples

- **Profit Models**: What are the different types of profit models for webinars?
- **Promise:** Why does a webinar pitch start with a promise?
- **Pacing:** How do you set the pace of your voice and energy, especially during the close?
- **Pitch Examples:** How do you use trial closes, decoys, stacking, proof, scarcity, clarity and closing statements to turn your webinar into a profit machine?

Pillar 7: PARTNER

Joint Ventures, Other People's Products

- **Joint Ventures:** Will your webinar offer benefit another company's customer base? Can you turn your competitors into partners?
- **Other People's Products:** How do you promote and profit from another company's product to license, present, and offer it on a webinar?

PILLAR 1: PERSPECTIVE

> ***"Your outlook affects your outcome."***
>
> *- John Paul Warren*

Passion, People, Purpose, Part

- **Passion:** What is it that you are teaching and sharing?
- **Purpose:** Where does the webinar fit in the overall scheme of your business?
- **People:** Who will benefit? Who are the other players?
- **Part:** What's your part? Which role(s) will you and other people perform?

A webinar is an event. A live event happens at a specific time. You must plot out your path to arrive at your desired outcome within the timeframe of the webinar. Your webinar must fit into your overall purpose for you and your company.

We talked about having a clear outcome for your webinar. Let's take a step back and get a higher perspective with a mental view or outlook. Your perspective is the big picture.

We'll look at the four areas of Perspective: Passion, Purpose, People and Part. *The Webinar Way* is not just about you running your own webinars to make money. There are many ways you can participate in the webinar experience.

What does PASSION have to do with WEBINARS?

People want enriching experiences. When presenting on a topic that you are passionate about, people *feel* it.

Jim Kukral, shares his webinar replay entitled *The New Rules of Self-Publishing* when you join the email club on his website. He is definitely passionate about self-publishing! His *Business Around A Book* website has a video replay on the homepage of his webinar on the subject.

A person who is truly passionate, and wishes to share their message using webinars, can reach global audiences to make a difference in the world. When we look at successful people who have changed the world (not necessarily with webinars) such as Mahatma Gandhi, Nelson Mandela, Richard Branson, Bono, and Steve Jobs, we often forget that, once upon a time, they were unknowns with little more than a dream. Remember the words of Earl Nightingale: "*Success is the progressive realization of a worthy ideal.*"

To borrow from entrepreneur Tony Hsieh in his book *Delivering Happiness,* the higher purpose type of happiness is being part of something bigger than yourself.

The three types of happiness are: pleasure (which can be fleeting); passion, which is peak performance because you are so engaged and in alignment with your actions; and higher purpose.

Your higher purpose is what you define. You may have lofty goals like President John F. Kennedy, who said, "*The only reason to give a speech is to change the world.*"

There are many webinars about learning how to live your life of passion conducted by personal development coaches. There are many webinars about turning your passion into profit. What you are sharing and teaching on your webinar is ideally in alignment with your passion because your audience will certainly feel it in your delivery!

To create a webinar presentation, we assume you have, at the minimum, the passion and knowledge about a particular subject. As we will discuss shortly, in the section on Parts you play in a webinar, you may be reading this book because you want to become a producer of webinars for people who are authorities in their marketplace and want to support these authorities, their passion and purpose. Or you are a passionate networker and want to be a webinar promoter (a.k.a. webinar broker) to get a piece of the action with a commission. Many people start off as an assistant on a webinar to see the inside of the process and the technology before conducting their own webinar.

If you don't have the passion part figured out, then you will probably benefit from Jim Kukral's second book in the *Business Around A Lifestyle* series. Volume 2 of the series is all about how to take the knowledge and passion that is in your head and turn it into an Internet business of some type. It doesn't matter who you are, or what you know a lot about, or what you're passionate about—you can build a business on the Internet. This volume goes into specifics and includes the how and why in complete detail, with examples.

Jim's premise is that from birth we're taught that we should all take a job just to make money. Because money equals happiness… right? Wrong. Money makes things easier, yes. But what makes us really happy is living the life we want, and the sooner you realize that the better.

The Webinar Lifestyle gives you a broad range of possibilities for your business, whether full-time or part-time. *The Webinar Lifestyle* gives you the type of freedom that perhaps you've dreamed about. This book will help make it a reality so that you can focus on what makes you really happy—living the life you truly want. When you are living the life you truly want, your passion is alive.

As a subject matter expert, it will be clear to your webinar participants if you have passion. It comes through your voice and the excitement you instill into your webinar presentation.

The PURPOSE of Your Webinar

> ***"Ideas can be life-changing. Sometimes all you need to open the door is just one more good idea."***
>
> *- Jim Rohn*

The purpose of your webinar may be to **increase your perception as an authority** and as a credible expert in your field. It may be to promote a new product or service. It may be to create a product from the webinar recording.

The purpose of your webinar can be big; it can be the main aspect of your business, or a part of your **business brand awareness**. Some people use webinars for **customer retention,** to answer questions to avoid returns, and maintain customer satisfaction. Others employ free webinars to **gather leads** and then **sell products and services**.

Your purpose may be **time-related**. To save yourself time, you'll want to skip straight to the automated webinar systems that we discuss in Part IV. Automated webinars mean that you respect the time of your target audience so they have the opportunity to schedule a time to watch and ask questions to be answered via email, often during or within a short time of the webinar conclusion.

Your purpose may be to **create a webinar series**. A webinar series needs a purpose with an overarching theme to tie all the webinars together. This theme message mirrors the big benefit. The title or headlines could start with the same words to create continuity. The purpose and theme of a webinar series has a storyline and creates mind-share in your intended audience. As Victor Hugo said, "*There is nothing so powerful as an idea whose time has come.*"

A webinar presentation can be a considerable test for a live speaking appearance, and your purpose may be to **test the audience reaction** and selling points, and to practice your delivery. That is one way to **get over stage fright** because you become so familiar with your material.

Get your webinar strategy in place before you start on your tactics. Your purpose is tied to your strategy.

Sherrie Rose and The Purpose of The Webinar Way

There is a purpose to this book, *The Webinar Way.* This is also where I tell you a little about me, Sherrie Rose.

If you've read this far in the book, you'll realize I have not talked much about myself. Stories are essential in webinars, but the TIMING of the story is also important.

In many webinars and books and stage presentations, the beginning is about "earning the right." This is the story of how they got started, made it big, are now successful and now have the right to teach you. Earning the right is the webinar presenter providing proof of their expertise along with images of checks with high dollar amounts, photos with celebrities, and images of them living *The Webinar Lifestyle* with fast cars in exotic locations.

If you don't have a co-host who introduces you on a webinar, please don't start by listing your credentials because your attendee's eyes will glaze-over and they'll lose interest if you start by talking all about you. They can't skip pages ahead as they can in a book. Give webinar participants actionable and value content right away. In free webinars, your primary purpose is to educate with valuable information that enriches and, hopefully, there is some entertainment value.

Now, with that out of the way, I can start talking about me, me, me! I love technology. All sorts of technology turns me on. Webinar technology turns me on.

I got started in Internet marketing in 2008. I loved the idea of using technology and making a profit. It was at Armand Morin's Big Seminar that was the genesis of my first business and product, when a fellow came in late and sat beside me in the back of the room. He was frazzled and I asked if everything was alright. He said he didn't think that he was going to make it to the seminar. I asked if he was sick. He said, "No, my wife was complaining that I was leaving again for another three-day weekend seminar." I leaned over and whispered, "If you filled her love bucket, she would be packing your suitcase, kissing you on the cheek and telling you to have a great time." He asked, "What's her love bucket?" I said, "I'll tell you on the break," and pointed to the stage in respect to Armand who was speaking.

At the end of the weekend, a group of us who had attended the seminar went out for dinner. The conversation turned to relationships and *her love bucket* came up. I was cajoled into explaining her love bucket. I did it reluctantly, and everyone said I needed to write a book, create a course, and sell it. So I did.

My very first interview was with Eben Pagan (a.k.a. David DeAngelo from Double Your Dating) on his Dating Guru Masters. He only did one more interview in his Mastery Series after me, because he wanted to focus on business coaching and put his dating and relationships products on auto-pilot. That one interview gave me immediate credibility and I hung up my shingle as *The Love Linguist.* I created other products on love, intimacy and relationships, and was a mentor.

I am a great networker and very good at understanding people. What was missing for me in the marketplace of love and intimate relationships was the technology aspect. I have a passion for technology, and it turns on my B-spot.

I talk more about the B-spot (brain + mind + emotions) in the Power Position Pillar. This is the psychology and impulses of what makes us do what we do. What does this have to do with webinars? You must connect and resonate with your audience through the B-spot to create and channel emotion on webinars, and to create sales. You need structure, content, and flowing sequence in your presentation all within the context of your topic.

I have always worked with software and systems. I am a systems person. I don't dive in completely until I have a better perspective on all the moving parts in the system. It is my purpose that the layout of this book will give you a systematic approach to webinars. As my colleague, Carlos Xuma, said about my approach to webinars, *"I love the way your left-brain works!"*

I had taken Armand Morin's speaker training called Persuasion X. This was designed for speaking from the stage and I could see how it directly related to webinar presentations. I also understood how the style elements and Internet marketing sales page played into a webinar presentation. Russell Brunson was also in that training and he went on to co-create Click Funnels as a landing page software that works great for webinar registration. Donna Fox who runs WebinarJam was also in attendance. We have a lot to be grateful for from Armand.

My first webinar experience, as an active participant, was with Armand Morin in 2008. I was in his mastermind group when he switched from the teleseminar audio-conference call format to webinars. He had not practiced and messed-up many places along the way. It shows that you just need to get started. If he was using his webinar as a selling mechanism, it would have been a disaster. Armand is now a webinar master and runs webinar conferences that he calls web camp.

I took it upon myself to become an expert in webinars. I studied webinars, learned more about webinar technology, became a webinar broker, and watched many webinars (while taking notes on so many errors and a few great tactics). I trained with the best and played many of the various roles in a webinar, as described in the section entitled Part later in Pillar I. I have been paid handsomely to coach people to improve their webinar presentations and conversions.

I checked out more webinar technology. Tying into *The Love Bucket,* one of the "rings of desire" is lifestyle. For me, just give me some great technology, because that fills my love bucket and also enhances my lifestyle. The technology part of webinars that many people have fears about is one of the things that I love. I discuss The Webinar Lifestyle in a later chapter.

Fast forward to a conversation I had with Brian Bagnall, Serial Entrepreneur and Webinar Expert. Brian and I met early in the year on the Marketer's Cruise. I created a webinar with Captain Lou Edwards. You can get details about the cruise and several more formats for automated webinars in Part IV, *The Webinar Lifestyle.*

Brian and I were talking about webinar technology and automated webinars. He told me about Casey Zeman's Easy Webinar and I was excited to try it. I had Hector Yague's system, the pre-cursor to Evergreen Business Systems, which eventually turned into Webinar Jam, Webinar Jam Studios, and EverWebinar. I loved the idea of people choosing a day and time that worked into their schedule instead of watching a 40-minute sales pitch video that had no viewer controls and no interaction. Casey's Easy Webinar was better than just a webinar replay, because the page layout was already designed and the attendee could ask questions in the chat area.

This book is also the basis for a full training program called *The Power of Webinars,* which combines technology and training in a webinar series and membership area. We use the foundation of the 7 Pillars and all of my proprietary tools for webinars. When you join the email list to get your free bonuses, you also get notified when registration opens for access to the membership area for more in-depth training. Inside is also the Fast Track M.A.P. (Massive Action Plan) that will help springboard your activity.

I've also interviewed successful webinar presenters, joint venture brokers, software creators and webinar participants. These free interviews are available on *The Webinar Way* website and the link is in the Webinar Resource Section of this book.

On *The Webinar Way* YouTube channel, there are over 40 videos from people who rave about using webinars in their business.

Webinars have been used for years in the Internet marketing space. I started noticing experts in various niches such as Real Estate, Local Business Consulting, Book Publishing, and Job/Resume Services offering to help other people with their webinars. They wanted well-trained webinar presenters so they could broker with them and provide a webinar that converts to their customer base. Partnering is Pillar 7 of *The Webinar Way.*

The purpose of *The Webinar Way* is to give you a great understanding of all the moving parts and remove as much of the surprise as possible with your webinar. It is filled with strategies and tactics from proven experts. There are ideas to help you get started, gather an audience, grow your customer base, turn your webinar into a profit machine and take action now. As Zig Ziglar says, "*You don't have to be great to start, but you have to start to be great.*"

PEOPLE

> ***"The Real Currency is Relationship Riches."***
>
> *- Sherrie Rose*

Life is about people and so is your webinar. It is about creating relationships and serving others. It is within those relationships that your riches flow, whether it's monetary riches from repeat buyers or intangible riches of residual rapport and recurring bonds with your fans and colleagues. Webinars give you the opportunity to touch the lives of people you will never meet and connect with persons all around the globe.

Honor your audience. Treat everyone with respect. All the people involved in the webinar, and the various parts and roles to be played, are breathing, heart-beating people. They are not numbers or statistics.

Webinars use the Internet to open a conversation with the right message about an excellent product or service, to the right people, at the right time. That's *The Webinar Way*!

If the real currency with people is relationship riches, in the world of webinars, the ultimate currency is experience. You create and provide the enriching experience through images and conversation. Tell your participants how they can act on your valuable content and create a webinar that outlines how you might be able to help them. A conversion-based webinar delivers actionable content and additional solutions beyond the webinar. You empathize and identify with their problem and you have a solution to offer. With webinars, you convert the conversation into currency.

Building relationships makes you money. A webinar is like making a phone call on a party line with everyone listening in. The number of people you connect with is directly correlated to your income. You want many people on your webinar.

A webinar gives you a platform to create a quality conversation with people in your target audience. If you have set up a survey to get feedback after your prospect registers, you now know what they need and how you can help, and then you can deliver the solution. Your survey may ask something along the lines of: "**What's your biggest problem**?" Recognize that you've got the solution they're looking for. When you close the right way on webinars, you make money.

If you don't have a webinar of your own, perhaps you've been on a webinar that you thought was fantastic. You can try your hand at becoming a webinar broker. Get on the phone with the person who hosted the webinar and let them know you want to promote them. You will have to get over any fears you may have and have a real person-to-person conversation.

Do your relationship building first. Everything else comes second.

With your webinar, when you share your expertise, you will gather an audience and create a following. People who resonate with you will come back to you. People will come back to you for more products and services and just to be your fan when you support their dreams, alleviate their fears, confirm their suspicions, identify the "bad guy" as your common enemy, and remove the fault from previous experiences. It is about building trust and rapport.

Who's Showing Up On Your Webinar?

"Preparation compensates for a lack of talent," says Joel Weldon, a member of the Speakers Hall of Fame.

In other words, you don't have to be the most talented. It's a matter of preparation: a) understanding your market (your audience), what their needs, wants and desires are, b) how you can specifically help them solve, satisfy, minimize, or eliminate their problems, challenges, or frustrations, and c) how you can most effectively present your solutions to them so they will not only "get it", but that they will then take action on what you gave them.

Know your customer. Appeal to their desires.

Create a short, accurate profile of the type of client you'd most like to attract. The people you want to attract, your prospects, need to be profiled. They need to have common identifiable issues, problems and habits. Define your audience by profiling. Create a profile of your intended target person to accurately predict and profile their characteristics to better address their unresolved issues, needs, wants and desires. This is their demographics and psychographics. Are you talking to men or women or both? Professional or novice? Married or dating? What is the root of their desire? This is a basic marketing exercise.

When you consider your profile or avatar, ask yourself what is happening in their personal or professional life. What would cause them to want what you are offering? You can have two people with the exact profile, but one wants to lose weight because of an upcoming high school reunion. There is motivation that is triggered by outside situations.

Get clear on the outcome. Know how you want the participants to think, feel or do, because they experienced your webinar.

Survey to profile your audience. Know their wants, needs, desires and wishes before the webinar. Define the path from where they are now and take them on the webinar experience to where you want to take them.

This list may seem similar to Maslow's Hierarchy of Needs of food, water, shelter and to avoid pain, but here is a quick list of what modern people are looking for:

- to be wealthy
- to be healthy
- to be good-looking
- to be popular
- to have celebrity
- to be seen as the authority
- to be part of an exclusive group
- to have freedom and free time
- to be of service others
- to feel inner peace
- to have fun

...and, the biggest one when it comes to the Internet is:

- to know how to do something the easiest, quickest, and cheapest way, with the greatest return on time and investment

Removing the frustration of your prospect by providing a solution, with a proven business system, is the most lucrative step that most of your prospects can take towards making a dream come true. Webinars are a system.

Create the profile for all the suspects in your target audience. When you know what the people in your target audience REALLY want then you can properly address their concerns, fears, hopes and desires. Your promotional messages and webinar content must resonate with the target audience.

When a person registers for a webinar, they have moved from suspect to prospect.

Previously, a webinar could have been considered a lead magnet or lead candy (much sweeter) on its own. Now you need a small offer to go along or precede the webinar. We will talk about this in the Promotion Pillar 3.

Who Are The Players in a Webinar?

You need perspective on the part, or parts, you will be playing in the webinar event. There are a lot of different roles to be played when putting on a webinar. You may be doing the webinar yourself and wearing multiple hats to produce your webinar. *The Webinar Way* is not just for the person who is conducting a webinar. *The Webinar Way* is for all the people who play various roles in the creation, coordination, promotion, and implementation of this technology.

All of the parts/roles noted below are not necessary and there are many overlapping tasks or different titles for the tasks to be performed. This is simply to give you more perspective. However you define the role you are playing, you will need to use a checklist. Part IV has the resources and checklists for you to run a successful webinar.

ON24, an enterprise-level webinar platform, breaks down the roles people play into four main areas: Producer (planning), Promoter (driving registration), Presenter (design and delivery), Video (live-casting and editing). Here's the expanded list:

Presenter: Who is the main presenter? Is this a solo act? What if someone doesn't show up; is there a backup plan? Is there a panel of speakers?

Host/Moderator/Facilitator: Introduces the guest speaker. Does the host, or an assistant, un-mute participants if you are opening up for questions or testimonials? Who will answer questions in chat while the webinar is going on?

Producer: Orchestrates everything for a successful LIVE webinar or skip right to producing an automated webinar.

Presentation Creator: Prepares the slides, writes the script and procures visuals (graphics, photos and images). Aligns the script with the timed agenda and includes allocating time for polls, drawing tools, and software demonstrations, etc.

Manager: Overall strategy. Manages the calendar of webinars, looks at trends and plans webinars, manages the budget, JV and affiliate payouts, and customer satisfaction.

Marketer: Handles promotion, publicity, social media, advertising, etc. to get registrations. Email marketing beforehand and after the webinar. Makes sure people show up for your webinar. Follow-up sequence and replays.

Coordinator/Assistant: Organizes and coordinates the logistics, keeping it all together while you conduct your webinar. Schedules dry-run beforehand to rally presenters and test webinar technology. Works with everyone on the support team.

Promoter/Broker: Puts deals together and gets a percentage of the sales. Finds a great product/service with a proven converting webinar. Introduces your webinar to another party with a matched target list of prospects and sets up meetings. See also Pillar 7, Partner.

Technical Support: Test the technology, the platform, hardware, software and equipment checks. Handles practice runs before, ensuring smooth operation during, and preparing the recording for an encore after the webinar event.

Web Support: Sets up the landing page funnels and campaigns for the webinar registration process, Thank You pages, order pages, bonus pages, and one-time offers, etc.

A/V Support: Handles video creation and editing for webinar promotion. Audio editing and video editing for webinar recording. Re-purposing audio and video content for sharing in various formats after the webinar.

Stakeholders: Who are the people who have the most to gain or who carry the most risk of loss when you plan your webinar?

Very likely, the main stakeholder is you, and you have many roles to play in your webinar. You have to decide how much of yourself you want in your webinar. Is it just slides with your voice commentary, or do you want to include your face on streaming video displayed in full or in a small corner of the screen? This choice will affect your decision for your webinar platform, too.

Determining the flow of your webinar presentation as well as who does what and when, will be key to a smooth event. If there are multiple people, know who opens with the welcome (sometimes called the webinar lobby) who is giving the introductions, who is giving the overview, who is running the polls, who is handling the Q&A session, and who is wrapping up your presentation.

If you want to play just one role, many of the other roles can be outsourced. You can hire experts or virtual assistants to handle various responsibilities for your webinar. Check the Resource Section of this book for places to get help.

A webinar is not a single event. It is part of your overall strategy. You or someone on your team should keep on top of trends and hot topics. Connect with industry thought leaders and develop relationships.

You may be reading this book because you want to become a webinar promoter, also known as a joint venture broker. You may become an exclusive webinar promoter for one joint venture partner. This can be a lucrative income, especially if you are a good networker and are good at spotting trends, and can cash in early.

You may be reading this book because you want to become a webinar manager at a company and want to know how to choose topics, locate webinar presenters, oversee marketing and registration and add webinars as a new profit center in your company.

You may be reading this book because you are excellent with graphics and visual presentation, and want to add webinar presentation creation to your set of valuable skills.

When you gain perspective on what role you want to play in the webinar, you will have a better handle on what needs to get accomplished. Take action and be persistent.

Calvin Coolidge said,"Nothing in the world can take the place of Persistence. Talent will not; nothing is more common than unsuccessful men with talent. Genius will not; unrewarded genius is almost a proverb. Education will not; the world is full of educated derelicts. Persistence and determination alone are omnipotent."

PILLAR 2: PLAN

> ***"Preparation Precedes Profit."***
>
> *- Sherrie Rose*

Platform, Planning, Process, Priorities

- **Platform:** What do you look for in webinar platform technology?
- **Planning:** Why does planning precede profit?
- **Process:** What do you include in your sales and marketing processes, campaigns, and funnels?
- **Priorities:** How do you determine your priorities in setting up and running a webinar?

Successful people plan and prepare. There are decisions to be made, steps to take, priorities, and an order to your webinar process.

Platform

Webinar platforms have evolved tremendously in the last few years. With newcomers, acquisitions, and anything software related, some go out of business. I recommend you do your homework before choosing the platform. There are over 40 webinar platform providers listed on *The Webinar Way* website along with their corresponding pricing. See the Resources section in Part V for the link.

When it is time to set up your webinar event from a technical perspective, think of it as you would prepare for a live in-person event. This set up includes webinar registration pages (funnel), webinar room set up for broadcasting and custom links. Take the time to think through how you want your webinar event to flow and set up the 'venue' correctly. Prepare any polls in advance. As you set up an individual webinar, you will want to ensure that you add your organizers, moderators, hosts and presenters with the appropriate access rights You will want to ensure that they receive the webinar details and are able to access the room ahead of the event flawlessly.

If you are new to webinars, we highly recommend getting a trial account to test the platform. Many webinar platforms start the billing cycle 14-30 days after signing up. Also you can try Zoom.us which is really built for video but can also be used successfully for webinars.

GoToWebinar (30-day trial) is an established platform in the Internet marketing circles, as well as Anymeeting (free with advertising). Three other well-known platforms are Adobe

Connect, Microsoft Live Meeting and Cisco WebEx. Google as a company uses ON24, but the price is pretty steep. Check to see if the webinar platform is browser-based or if a download is required.

Google+, the Google social platform, introduced "Hangouts," originally for 10 people. They have expanded this to "Hangouts on Air" to broadcast yourself to people around the air. These are free. You can use YouTube Live to create a Quick event with Hangouts on Air, or a Custom event using an encoder. Invite friends or clients to participate. You can embed your live broadcast on your blog or website, or participants can watch on your YouTube channel. Your webinar recording will then be uploaded to your YouTube account.

Several webinar platforms have incorporated Google Hangouts on Air. Some of these are replacing Hangouts on Air because this is a time delay that affects performance.

Some webinar platforms are already integrated with Facebook Live and YouTube Live, bringing your content to social media for additional promotion.

Listen to *The Webinar Way* interview with Jay Kubassek, who switched from GoToWebinar to MeetingBurner. Jay said during his interview, *"This could be a sales pitch for MeetingBurner."* Also listen to the interview with Kimberly Castleberry who goes into detail on what you need to know about the features of MeetingBurner. Unfortunately, *MeetingBurner closed in December 2017* after seven years of quality service. MeetingBurner relied heavily on Adobe Flash technology that is not keeping up with the modern Internet so Paul Rydell decided to close it down.

From the participant's point of view, a survey conducted by the 1080 Group found that "ease of use" of the webinar platform was cited as a top success factor when joining or participating on a webinar.

Features to look for in your webinar platform are:

1. A cost and technology model that makes it easy to present to 10 participants, or scale to 1000 webinar attendees or more
2. The ability to see who is present and attentive
3. The ability to record and have on-demand or auto-pilot webinars within hours of the webinar event
4. The capacity for easy interaction, including questions, chat, muting attendees, opening up phone lines for live audio questions
5. Several methods to connect via phone, Skype, and web browser
6. An easy-to-manage dashboard to set-up presenter profiles, registration pages, and payments for paid webinars
7. The capacity for speakers to share their desktops, slides, various files, applications, web pages and membership sites

Top-notch webinar presenters go beyond understanding the basic functionality of the webinar platform they use. More knowledge gives you the power to produce riveting experiences, which boosts your brand, reputation and generates higher quality leads. Shelby Britton suggests you dig in deep and become a power user of the technology, pushing it to its limits and finding new and unique ways to use the product to engage their audience.

Here are some of the things you can look for in a webinar platform:

- Instant Screen Sharing or Webinar Scheduling
- Streaming Video of Host
- Audio Conferencing (Telephone, Computer, Skype)
- Mobile Attendee Support
- Instantly Change Presenters
- In Meeting Chat (public)
- In Meeting Questions (private)
- Customizable Meeting Registration Page
- Automated SMS Reminders
- Automated Email Reminders
- Meeting Recording
- Recorded Meeting Sharing
- Automated Meetings
- Hybrid Webinars
- Meeting Analytics
- Payments with PayPal Integration
- Mac & PC Compatible
- Share mobile screens from your phone or tablet.
- Support via phone and email

Mari Smith, who wrote the forward to *The Webinar Way*, says using the webcam to LiveStream, as a live video webcast format, helps promote her personality-based brand and connect more with her online attendees because it can handle tens of thousands of viewers. There are other high definition live video webinar options that allow charismatic speakers and presenters to connect effectively and develop relationships with the participants. The chat feature in these environments must be moderated by someone other than the presenter.

The latest WebinarNinja platform combines webinar software, registration page software, email marketing and video recording. To edit the webinar, you have two options: Basic & Advanced. Use simple opt-in to edit the 'basic details' of your webinar (date, time etc.). Use Advanced to add your style and customize your webinar pages. Change colors, fonts, template, and more. Additionally, you can clone to duplicate and create a replay. WebinarNinja is a very fast set-up.

There are also Facebook apps that are designed for webinars. Newer platforms are available such as Blink Webinars, Zoom.us, Click Webinar, Join.me, CrowdCast.io and Demio. Be warned that there are often early development technical bugs, so presenter beware. Depending on the level of experience and trust of your target audience, these webinar platforms may or may not work for you.

Focus on the participant experience. How easy is it to access the webinar? Have you eliminated any frustrating elements that could affect the participant's mood or that may impact your desired outcome? Make sure the platform preserves the quality of your slideshows. If you are using streaming, make sure it delivers high-quality live video that does not distort the face of your presenters.

Most webinar systems offer a conference bridge line in addition to web broadcast audio. Some, international participants and even webinar panelists prefer to call in by phone.

Whichever platform you choose, get practice to learn how to use it well and how to leverage its tools. Some providers have webinar services to assist you throughout the process of preparing a webinar in addition to the technology. It is worth practicing, at least a few times, with those providers that provide free service or 30-day trials, until you master the platform. Ideally, you choose a webinar platform based on your ROE (return on event), which you can determine with the metrics using *The Webinar Way Profit Calculator*, especially if you are delivering webinars for sales purposes.

Testing and practicing all the features of the platform is crucial. Put in the time to master the technology. Try out all the buttons and get very familiar with features, so you stay in the control position.

We will be discussing automated webinar platforms in Part V, in the section on Perpetual Profits.

PLANNING

> ***"I'm going to give a long speech today. I haven't had time to prepare a short one."***
>
> *- Professor Alden*

Planning your webinar is a piece of cake if you've done it before. It is kind of like driving a car. If you've done it for years, it is second nature. When you are starting out learning how to drive, you need to take it step by step and make sure you don't step on the gas when you mean to step on the brake, or go in reverse instead driving forward. Some of it is technology, some of it is practice, and a lot of it is following your plan.

U.S. President Woodrow Wilson was once asked how long it took him to write a speech. He answered, *"That depends. If I am to speak ten minutes, I need a week for preparation. If fifteen minutes, three days; if half an hour, two days; if an hour, I am ready now."* The tighter and more concise your presentation, the longer it takes to prepare. In an ideal world, you should give yourself 6-8 weeks to plan for the logistics and prepare your webinar presentation, if you are starting from scratch. At a minimum, you need one week before the webinar. Add one week after the webinar for follow-up. Planning puts you in the driver's seat to mitigate problems.

I've seen ad hoc, spur of the moment webinars. This is often for software demonstrations with questions and answers for an existing customer base, and not for a presentation-style webinar designed for the purpose of selling. The planning in this case is the expert knowledge and steps for the software demonstration.

Refer to your desired outcome and start with the end in mind. Give yourself a deadline, even if it is your first dry run with only your mother as your audience member. Set your goals for each and work backwards from there. If you find yourself going in circles, it's because you don't have a clear, specific target that has a deadline.

As mentioned before, a webinar is an event and has the elements of a product launch. You need to plan each step. Some steps happen simultaneously, some steps happen in tandem.

We just talked about platform, but there are other techware (technology + software) decisions that you may want to plan for. The webinar event is a launch which includes adding SMS text messages to the registration process, customized registration pages, plans for doing live demos during the presentation, etc.

Take a look again at the 3C by 3T Matrix, figure 3. It is a smart move to get your resources organized in T1 before your webinar goes live. Your budget, presenters, promotion, messages, event coordination, and many other logistics all need to be put in place. Good preparation, a good moderator, rehearsals, and a good marketing promotion plan will help build momentum.

Determine where webinars fit into your marketing plan: First, where in your content marketing mix do webinars fit best for your unique customer engagement cycle? Second, use webinars for brand recognition, better content memorability, and when appropriate for sales. Then add determine where the webinar will fit within the overall marketing funnel (top of funnel, middle of funnel, bottom of funnel). For example, consider the timing of a thought leader webinar for prospect acquisition. This type would probably go at the top of your engagement funnel while a product demo webinar would go near the bottom after the prospect has some familiarity with your business.

Some webinar planning pointers:

- Create and manage a webinar calendar. Follow the 3C by 3T matrix to track promotions, webinar topics, titles, presenters, future webinars, etc.
- Create a marketing plan for each webinar. Whether it is a one-time webinar, a series of webinars, or a demo webinar, prepare in advance the summary, data, and information for your joint venture partners.
- Size does matter. The more targeted audience members you can attract the more conversions from registrant to revenue. Improve and expand your marketing and test new avenues.
- Email or CRM capabilities. Integrate your webinar registrants' email and attendee data into an auto-responder or (CRM) customer relationship management

system to manage your opt-in list. Generating leads is one of the key goals of webinars.

- If it works, do it again. Once you have a converting webinar, plan on doing it again. Perhaps with a JV partner or offer it as an upsell or bonus to a complimentary list owner. Keep track of and reuse the tactics that made it successful. You owe it to a new audience to captivate, educate and enrich them with your webinar presentation.

A dozen or more problems can occur on a webinar. You need a back-up plan, a Plan B. You can lose your place and forget what you're talking about, which is embarrassing, but is fairly easy to get over.

Problems can come in the form of your guest speaker not showing up, or perhaps you get laryngitis and can't talk on the scheduled day. It could be technical if you lose your sound or video feed, or your webinar platform does not work, or your participants could drop off unexpectedly. It is always good to have a back-up computer. Some people suggest using two monitors. My friend Harlan Kilstein is a Mac lover, but always uses a PC for his webinars.

You have to be ruthless with your time. If any distractions get in your way, you have to be ruthless with them, too. Know what needs prioritizing. Use the checklists to keep yourself on track.

Planning your Equipment

The basics: A computer and webinar platform software. A laptop, desktop, PC or Mac plugged-in (not on battery). Start with a free or trial service for your webinar platform.

Optional equipment is an external microphone such as recommend the Audio Technica ATR-2100 USB microphone. A boom arm for the microphone. A webcam, if you are live streaming. Headphones are highly recommended to keep external audio in your ears so you do not cause an echo for your audience.

For your slides, you can use PowerPoint, Keynote or Google Slides or others. Google Slides is free with any Gmail account, and you collaborate with others, save your presentations in the cloud and export slides as a PowerPoint file.

The webinar platform software usually comes with a registration page and ideally statistics and analytics. The pages you will need are the registration page, the thank you page, and optional replay page. You'll also want email confirmations and reminders.

Planning with People

Get together with the "cast and crew" of your webinar. Work with the behind-the-scenes helpers if you have them and define their roles. Big webinar events require a team. If your JV partner promises several hundred attendees, you should plan for at least one webinar moderator/assistant for every 50 attendees to help with answering the questions.

One financial expert holds several joint venture webinars a month. He created an extensive checklist identifying the task, role/person, and even the software associated with that person's responsibility. Software often comes with access and passwords, so working with people you trust is critical.

Hold a pre-webinar conference call and make sure you are on the same page with your moderator. Get clear on how to answer questions. Know what questions you'd like to be asked and what questions you would like to avoid. Make your webinar interactive with quality questions.

Identify what types of questions can be asked live on behalf of the attendees by the moderator, what types of comments to share, and list "seeded" questions in case the question or objection is not asked. The moderator can also provide the order link to the sales page in the chat box, at the end of the webinar. Identify common questions and have these posted on the webinar; if someone is thinking of it and you are addressing it, they don't feel like they are alone. Everyone benefits from addressing common objections and concerns.

Plan to be ready early. Give yourself and your team a 24-48 hour rule. If you are working with a co-presenter or moderator, use Dropbox, Google Drive, or something similar to share your presentation in advance. Save your final draft and create a copy with a different name. You never know if a file has become corrupted. Upload the final version and test it.

Process

> ***"Airplane Pilots who believe in checklists usually use flow patterns and mental checklists to prepare an airplane for a specific task; they then back up those actions with the appropriate written checklist."***
>
> *- Ralph Butcher*

A webinar is an exciting process that is a collection of interrelated tasks and activities that relate to each other through sequence and flow. The completion of one action flows into the initiation of the next step. Use a pre-webinar checklist like a pilot's checklist before take-off. Create as many checklists as you need to stay organized and on task. There are checklists for each Pillar in the Power of Webinars training program.

REMINDER: If you skipped the Webinar Quick Start, go back and read the WAMO Approach and the 3T by 3C Matrix. We refer to the matrix in figure 3 several times.

The WAMO Method is an initial process. The 3C by 3T Matrix is another process. Completing your "Persuasion Map" is yet another process.

The 7 Pillars of The Webinar Way are a process. Ideally, you will create custom process maps, mind maps, sequences, checklists and flow charts. Decide on each step of the process. For example, at the time of registration, add a relevant custom question to the registration fields. By doing so, you show them you care about your attendees' concerns because you're gathering useful information to use during the live presentation. Or, when they complete the registration, take them to a quick survey with 3-5 questions. Also, conversions are much higher when you offer two times for the webinar on the registration page. For example, you can offer the same time 5:00PM for both the East and Pacific Time zones.

There are several process examples that were found freely available on the Internet. They are in the Resource Section of this book and included for your use.

Kevin Riley of *Kevin Riley Publications* gave his permission to share his joint venture process map. This process will work for your own communications. There is a link in the Resource Section for full details. Kevin is a man to watch. His process map is colored-coded and is very well laid out. It includes:

- (7) Pre-written emails sent prior to the webinar event

- (8) Web pages (pre-sell, webinar registration, social proof, etc.)
- Bonus Giveaway (digital) a.k.a lead candy
- (5) videos on various pages
- (1) video on each order page and webinar replay page
- (15) system emails for follow-up

Kevin is extremely successful and has perfected his Internet marketing craft and webinar system. His process map does not include the detail of the emails or web page content, but rather a great overview process of the information flow. His process map includes the timing of the emails.

The cool kids are now calling the process map a "campaign" or a "funnel." It does not matter what the label is, the elements are the same. Copy, images, CRM, web pages, and lead candy gifts in any format will comprise the elements of your process. Note: These terms: process, campaign and funnel usually represent the same steps.

You will want to develop your own processes and checklists. For our clients, we use over 39 pages of checklists for the 7 Pillars. Each of the 7 Pillars has a 3-8 page checklist and Pillar 4 has two checklists. These checklists are part of the Power of Webinars training program. Customize your checklists for your own needs and style.

Priorities

> ***"I can't change the direction of the wind, but I can adjust my sails* to always reach my destination."***
>
> *- Jimmy Dean (*sales)*

Use the 3C by 3T matrix to help plan your priorities. Some things are dependent on other things happening first. Here is a sample schedule over a 30-day period. You may plan your webinar 6-8 weeks out. You may plan to do an impromptu webinar. Define your priorities based on the desired outcome you have set for your webinar.

You can start planning a webinar launch three months before it happens live. It is an event and timing depends if this is a new launch or a re-run of an existing webinar launch campaign.

Yes, you CAN create, set-up, and run a webinar in 29 days or less. If you are just starting, give yourself at least 45 days.

SAMPLE SCHEDULING FOR WEBINAR

T1 Pre-Webinar

Days 1-24

Planning, Promoting, Preparing

Day 1: WAMO Approach – Is a webinar the right tool for your message? Is your offer ready for the webinar close?

Day 2-5: Where is the audience? What lead candy (gift) will attract your audience?

Day 5-10: Plan for the webinar platform, people, logistics, equipment, tools and practice sessions. Are your resources in place? Are your timelines set? Are pages and funnels built?

Day 10-15: Set-up promotion. Take survey (optional)

Day 15-22: Review registrations and prepare to revise content based on survey results. Review and update internal communications and prospect email messages.

Day 23: Final technology test, complete practice, and firm established Power Position.

Day 23-24: Mission Ready Checklist – 2 days before.

T2 Webinar EVENT

Day 25

PRESENTATION DAY

Just prior: *Webinar GO-Live Checklist:* Webinar Event Day Quick Reminders

After webinar: Review – Plug-in your metrics into *The Webinar Way Profit Calculator*

T3 Post-Webinar

Days 26-30

Follow-Up Process

Day 26: Email follow-up to participants and non-attendees. Options to send transcripts, summary notes, or other promises.

Day 27-30: Replay, reminders, special offers, upsells, and downsells

Day 27-30: Review feedback, social media, email, chat, metrics and stats, debrief with team

Test your promotional messages for impact and revise if necessary. One of the most important priorities is practice. Practice includes testing the webinar platform and rehearsing your presentation. Practice also includes having a "meet and greet" with your joint venture partner and discussing the transitions so you don't talk over one another. Practice is also testing all the equipment. Practice is testing your supporting web pages and links. Practice is testing the webinar platform, the emails, and SMS alerts.

No matter how good the webinar platform, you should learn how to use it well and know how to leverage its tools. Practice with the same computer, audio headset and internet access that you will use on the day of the webinar event. Practicing your delivery style via the new virtual environment will help increase your comfort level. This element is crucial even if you've presented the same content in other settings. You will also want to go through your slide deck to make sure they look nice in the virtual webinar so they go smoothly and seamlessly in practice and on the day of the event.

Allocate time in your schedule for practice, rehearsals, dry runs and testing. Preparation is an important key to success.

If you are planning to become a master of webinars, you must be ready to review your performance, check your metrics, make adjustments, and prepare to improve. Continuous improvement of your webinar helps you tap into bigger paydays, and even the massive potential power of a webinar series.

Accept things may go wrong. No matter how much you plan and prepare, things can – and will – go wrong. Don't stress over things that occur during the live event. Chris McHale had a presenter who was using his laptop to present. The scheduled presenter didn't plug the laptop in using the power cord and was running off the battery which cut out. They were about 10-20 minutes into the presentation when his presentation went black. The laptop ran out of power and the computer shut right off. Chris unexpectedly shifted from moderator to the presenter and had to 'entertain' the audience for about ten more minutes as the scheduled presenter had to get his power cord, sign back in and resume where he had left off in the presentation.

Persist Beyond Exception: A webinar and the surrounding plan is a system that can create income and financial freedom. Stick with your plan at the same time you rearrange your priorities to perfect your webinar and become a master. Listen to *The Webinar Way* interview with Danny Iny about making iterative changes to your presentation. Make adjustments to your webinar presentation. You will always come out ahead.

Planning and Profits: Whoever said "cash flow follows the calendar" is right. You must plan your webinar, plan your promotion, tie it all into an implementation calendar and marketing calendar. You need a promotion calendar, which we talk about next.

PILLAR 3: PROMOTE

> ***"Good promotion creates a reaction."***
>
> *- Jim Kukral*

Promotion, Pages, Proof, Pre-sell

- **Promotion:** What are the different ways to promote a webinar?
- **Pages:** What types of web pages are needed for the various aspects of a webinar?
- **Proof:** Why do testimonials and other forms of proof attract webinar registrations?
- **Pre-sell:** How do you pre-sell with benefits and create "hooks?"

Many webinar producers focus on the webinar event. Giving attention to creating a marketing plan designed to reach a large group of prospective registrants is a key to a successful webinar.

Many webinar presenters focus on crafting a stellar presentation. Yes, you need one. But without proper promotion, who will watch it and take you up on your offer?

Often, advertising promotion targets colder traffic, so you have to get them on an email list and warm them up with content-rich email messages before the webinar event. The takes planning and time.

To drive webinar registrations, a targeted communication in a focused email invitation works better than most any other promotional tactic

Some people don't start to promote until they have their webinar presentation completed. If you are clear on your message, you can start promoting in advance. If you are a procrastinator, start promoting and you will see how quickly your presentation gets completed!

PROMOTE EVERYWHERE

Join the Webinar Marketing Groups on Facebook and Google+ to share ideas and learn more about webinar promotion: http://MarketYourWebinars.com.

Free methods of promoting:

- Your existing Email List of prospects and customers
- Video promoting the webinar on YouTube
- Video promoting the webinar on your Registration Page
- Video promoting the webinar on your Facebook Page

- Live video service: Facebook Live
- Live video service: Snapchat
- Live video service: Periscope
- Create a Facebook Event
- Write a note on your Facebook Page
- Add links to the registration page on your Facebook Page and Groups
- Use a Twitter service to set up a series of tweets
- Write posts on Google +
- Video promoting the webinar on Google +
- Write posts on your Google + page
- Add a LinkedIn event
- Create a LinkedIn Group
- Write a blog post
- Write a guest blog post
- Write a free report to give away
- In interviews, include news of upcoming webinar events
- Listings in webinar directories
- Create a Google+ Event
- Add links to registration page in Google+ Communities
- Add images with registration link on Pinterest

Sean Malarkey, who was kind enough to provide a video on *The Webinar Way* YouTube Channel and a quote in the "*In Praise of Webinars*" section at the beginning of the book, has this advice to share: "Be different." Steve Jobs of Apple used a similar theme: "Think different."

Sean tested two things very differently than normal and the results speak for themselves. The first resulted in a 75% opt-in rate for a webinar through the first 4,000 clicks. Normally the registrations hover around 55%. The second thing that was different after the change was an up-sell that normally converted at 23% now converted at 47% through the first 100 sales.

It doesn't matter what each thing was specifically. The idea is to be different—test new things. Don't be afraid to go against everything you know and trust your gut if you think it might work!

PAGES, PROOF, PRE-SELL: Promotion Content – Pre-Webinar

The primary purpose of your webinar invitation is to "sell" your webinar. In the past, a webinar invitation to a cold audience was good enough. Now, with so much competition in the marketplace, you need to entice them with more. Offer a gift, (lead candy, lead magnet, gateway gift) as an optional first step.

Why do you need the first step? It has to do with the attention span of our prospective webinar attendee. To get the registration, you first need to offer something that is highly desired and easy and fast to see and consume.

Choosing and naming your lead candy is critical in getting people to opt-in on your landing page. Lead candy consumption must be fast and easy. There is a time and place for all types of lead magnets and choosing the order you offer them is critical. You need to test. Lead candy should attract suspects like bees to honey ... having them sign up in droves. If you're a coach or consultant, use these steps: 1) entice with a lead candy digital download on an opt-in page, 2) give webinar invitation on the Thank You page (with or without video; this gives time to build trust and have prospects get to know you), or 3) run a live webinar and, since you have warmed them up, at the end is the time to offer a free consultation strategy session.

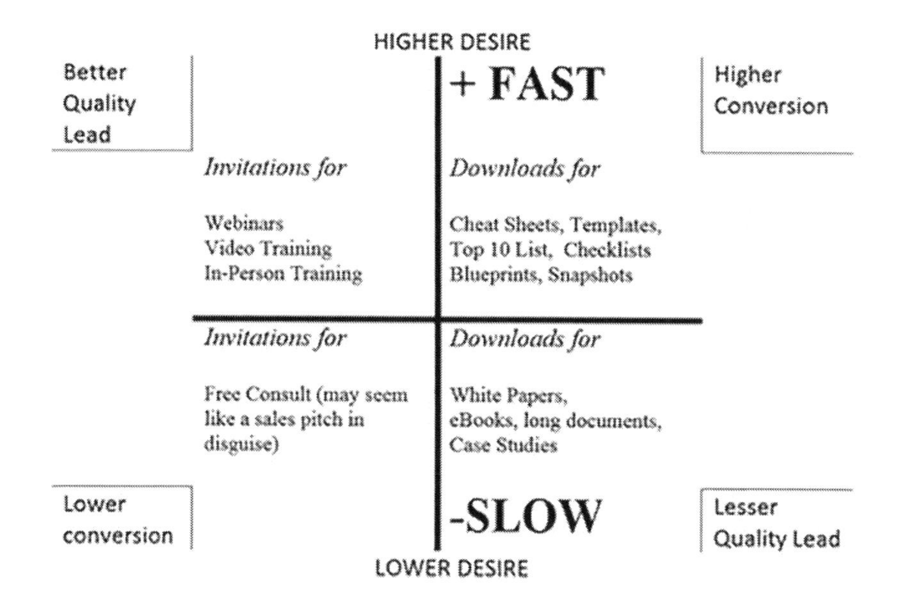

Figure 5

You can invite people directly to your webinar if you have an existing list of subscribers. If not, then offer the lead candy download first followed by the webinar. Lead candy gift is easily digestible and makes prospects hunger for more. The more your webinar provides, the "more" they are craving. Can ycn promote it together, so they get the lead candy (either download on Thank You page or via email) and automatically get registered on the webinar. If you invite them to the webinar only on the Thank You page after receiving the gift, you can do this with text or video. Yes, it seems like it is getting more complicated, and it is.

Several years ago it was easier to get someone to sign up on a webinar. Now, because the time commitment is seen upfront as a detractor, the first step is to offer the lead candy. This makes someone more open to the idea of the webinar relating to the lead candy.

There are several options, but two main players, in the opt-in and registration page SaaS (software as a service) marketplace. One is called LeadPages and the other is Click Funnels. According to Leadpages, webinar registration pages typically have a 30% conversion rate. Others are Unbounce, OptimizePress, 10 Minute Funnels, Lander, Instapage, and Pagewiz. These have multiple predesigned registration pages where all you need to do is change text, add an image (optional), connect to your email autoresponder or CRM and link your terms and privacy pages. They offer Thank You pages, survey pages, order forms and more. Great for split testing. This is a big time saver in setting up your webinar registration.

One point about mobile. Mobile access is huge and these services have responsive, mobile-optimized pages. If you use custom registration pages, they must work on mobile.

Go to Leadpages to see a demo of landing pages being built before your eyes. There are many visual examples of various webinar registration pages, advertisements, and related promotional pages on *The Webinar Way* Pinterest boards.

http://pinterest.com/thewebinarway/

Create continuity in the look and feel between your various pre-webinar web pages, such as web landing page, registration page, Thank You page, etc. Ensure the registration and login page(s) are consistent with your visual identity. Your webinar platform should enable you to quickly customize your webinar registration and "event room." Incorporate your defined purpose and outcome, and view your webinar environment as an extension of your main website or project-specific web pages. With the landing page builders, this is easy. If you have your own web programming team, they can do this right on your website with either custom programming with the landing page builder options that let you publish to a WordPress site or download the HTML code.

The new video formats such as Facebook Live, Periscope, Snapchat and others get in the news stream and you can have in immediate connection with your potential webinar audience.

Your YouTube channel is also a great place to start the story of your webinar and begin promotion. Video is a great way to create a connection and build rapport. Include the right content with hooks and get them to close by clicking on the link provided that takes them to the next step.

A registration page tells the story of your webinar. Whichever route they arrived, it now gives the visitor the option to decide if they will enter their name and email address. Make the registration easy. A video on the registration page enhances the story.

Don't be lazy and choose a generic registration page that comes with your webinar platform. Add some "flavor" with a logo and photo of the presenter(s). There are so many ways to test your page with different profiles, logos, text, images, compelling copy in bullet points, etc. Remember to add your terms and conditions and privacy links.

Give the webinar registration the proper cosmetic attention and have your graphic designer help with images to create a space that reflects the experience you want. You may be able to add a color theme or skin to the webinar platform. Customization is more than just your logo. If your registration page software allows, include share buttons for Twitter, Facebook, Google+, LinkedIn and other social networks to get viral promotion. Social sharing may be best on your Thank You page.

More Pages. Your webinar registration page can be a customizable WordPress plugin. These types of plugins give you the ability to double-deliver email addresses into both the webinar platform registration system and your email follow-up system. Include a Thank You page or survey upon completion of the registration. If you add an upsell at this stage, also include a Thank You page for the upsell. Map-out any custom types of web pages that are needed for the various aspects of your webinar.

Proof. If you have bona fide testimonials in text or video, including them on your registration Thank You page for great social proof. Testimonials help to establish your authority and Power Position. Case studies showing steps and results are powerful proof in your webinar and there may be a small piece that can be included in the webinar invitation.

Pre-sell. Pre-selling identifies benefits and creates "hooks" based on the interests and desires of your attendees. Create a great title and email subject lines for your webinar.

A possible pre-sell addition: If you have a previous webinar, turn small snippets into a video. This makes it easy to digest and consume. What are the easy and logical segments that will have an impact? This can be a teaser for the main webinar event.

Post-Sell. Post-selling happens after your webinar in T3 on the 3Cx3T matrix. You continue to promote your webinar value and ideas with a clear email and follow-up campaign. Follow-up is step 5 of the Five Ups, figure 1.

Quick Tips To Close More Sales After Your Webinar

Customize your email follow-up campaigns for these audiences:

1. People who completed the entire webinar but did not take action
2. People who left the webinar early
3. People who registered but didn't attend the webinar
4. Curate an ongoing audience to build more rapport

Optional Extras and Social Follow-Up

- Always keep an automated webinar or replay available.
- Upload your presentation/presentation slides through Slideshare on Linkedin.
- Create a transcript of the webinar and share it with your audience.
- Upload webinar image on Google images.
- Upload webinar images on Pinterest.
- Create retargeting ads for people who didn't show up and personalize the ad for them.
- Email sequence in an automated campaign for the ads.
- Automate or send messages through LinkedIn and Facebook Messenger (Chat bot such as ManyChat give a a personal style communnication) and LinkedIn.

WEBINARA PROMOTION COMMUNITY

Webinara (www.webinara.com) is a social-media driven community that helps hosts promote webinars and pairs attendees with webinars that are most relevant to them.

Webinara addresses two primary challenges:

1. There are many good webinars hidden from view and easy discovery, and

2. All webinar organizers want more attendees.

How Webinara Works

Most industries and topics (including both corporate and personal interest/educational webinars) are listed. Each event listing is tagged by the organizer with up to three categories. The members of the Webinara community who are subscribed to those categories are notified when there is an upcoming webinar matching their areas of interests.

Webinara actively promotes each webinar throughout social media to help spread the word and increase the brand awareness and thought-leadership of host companies.

The Webinara Value Proposition

Webinara complements traditional marketing channels like email lists, websites, social media, and partner co-promotion. When an organizer is posting a webinar, Webinara leads them through a guided process that places a particular focus on 'what's in it for the attendee'. Webinara automatically creates a company profile page and a webinar landing page, both of which are searchable in Google and include information about how to optimize listings for SEO. Webinara also allows hosts to communicate with attendees before and after the webinar. When the webinar is over, the recording can be added to the event listing and the webinar becomes available on-demand for future viewers.

Webinara integrates with the majority of webinar solutions on the market, which makes the registration process seamless and centralizes the critical traffic and CRM data associated with each event. All other webinar solutions can also be used as long as there is a webinar registration page. Webinara also offers webinar statistics and the opportunity to track and improve attendance over time as well as webinar consulting/coaching services and a webinar blog.

Since launching in 2015 as a tech startup based in Norway, Webinara has expanded and is now also incorporated in the United States and in India (2017) and their team of marketers, designers, and developers has attracted over 800 companies worldwide that promote their webinars and grow their audience.

7 WAYS TO CREATE A SEDUCTIVE WEBINAR TITLE

Webinars with seductive titles attract more people. The most useful information on a webinar will not be seen or heard if the title of your webinar is boring. The more actionable the title, the better. The webinar title should answer the question, "What will I get by giving you an hour of my time and attention?"

This is basic copywriting 101: start with a powerful headline. Here are seven steps to make the titles of your webinars more catchy, powerful and seductive:

1. **Start with the words "How to."** Starting with "How to" implies you will be training and teaching people exactly how to do whatever it is that you promise. And

they'll need several of examples, too. Example: "How to Create a Seductive Webinar Title."

2. **Start with an action verb.** Example: "Create a Seductive Title for Your Webinar: Secrets from the Masters." An action word like "create" instantly engages the mind and the imagination of the prospective webinar registrant.

3. **Follow the action verb with the intended outcome of your webinar.** "Create Seductive Webinar Titles To Attract Bigger Audiences." This title makes it clear to the prospective attendees by answering the question, "What's in it for me?" If a bigger audience is important to them then they will register for the webinar.

4. **Add in searchable keywords.** If you're promoting your webinars online, your webinar title needs to be searchable. Do some keyword research and make it seductive for Google, Yahoo, Facebook and other search engines.

5. **Start with an odd number.** Numbers under ten work better than larger numbers and odd numbers are more magnetic than even numbers. Three, five and seven are popular starting numbers. An example: "7 Ways To Create Amazing Webinar Titles To Attract The Right Audience And Get Sign-Ups." This example includes an odd number, an active verb, searchable key works and the intended outcome. The desired outcome is what you define in your WAMO Approach.

6. **Use words like "Steps."** Steps, Ways, Methods, Systems, and Blueprints are words that indicate you will be laying out the exact steps to follow on your webinar.

7. **Get to the point, fast.** Create a title that catches people's attention in a few short words and gets them to read your entire webinar description. The title needs to be clear and concise, and appeal to the intended audience and their needs or interests. Test out different versions and then go with the best converting title.

WEBINAR INVITATION COMPONENTS

Headline (Connection). As noted above, the primary benefit is the headline. The headline is the most important contact to get attention. Test several. Just as important as the headline is the subject line of email messages, Facebook event headlines and blog headlines about the webinar. Create a hypnotic headline that creates curiosity and draws in your audience.

Marketing Copy (Content). Create interest with secondary elements such as what attendees will learn, what questions they will be able to ask, what they will see, what they will experience, and what they can expect during the webinar. The content is also designed to create a connection with the presenter. This is where you are educating the prospective attendee on the benefits of the webinar. Include questions, an example or story, bullet point format, and especially effective is a burning problem that your target audience faces. Summarize these benefits in 3-7 short phrases.

Webinar Offer and Call to Action (Close). The content and connection is part of the build-up to the close. The description of the webinar includes the title, timing, presenter(s), and bonuses for registration or attending the webinar. The offer also includes whether this is a free or paid webinar. To guarantee your webinar has a high attendance rate, use the power of an irresistible offer by describing one or more coveted free bonuses for registering that will be received immediately.

A Note about Content. Be sure that your webinar invitation supports the value you are promoting. If you are creating the buzz and hype, be prepared to deliver. In fact, over-deliver on your promise. Content encompasses the "what you will get" and supports the "what's in it for me" that the registrants are responding to in your invitation. Know what they are likely to want to see and learn with polls, surveys and questions. Make sure your promotion and what you deliver are in-sync. There's nothing worse than a "bait and switch" on a webinar, even if it is unintended.

How I Turned A Losing Webinar Into A Multi-million Dollar Success

My friend Caleb O'Dowd shared a post entitled "HOW I MADE $363,000 IN 4 DAYS", and how he had success in launching a new webinar in January.

What most folks don't know, though, is that Caleb actually launched that webinar a few months earlier but couldn't get it off the ground.

Yes, he had success with a JV or two. But overall, the appeal didn't hit a nerve… and therefore… it died a fast death.

He initially entitled it The Newspaper Profit Formula.

The gist of the positioning was that newspaper advertising was easier, cheaper and more profitable than Google, Facebook and YouTube traffic. The appeal was too direct or else too "alien" for most. Sadly, people didn't bite.

So the job became to reposition the webinar target a different prospect in the marketplace warm folks up to the newspaper advertising idea and then lower the boom and sell them into the program.

The new positioning and title became The Supplement Business Launch Formula.

This was a radically different position than the previous one. And yet, the webinar training content was exactly the same. The results between the two were astonishing.

While *The Newspaper Profit Formula* bombed… *The Supplement Business Launch Formula* took off like a rocket and made Caleb millions upon millions of dollars.

Over the years, Caleb learned the skill of turning losers into winners and winners into even bigger winners. So, it doesn't matter how great your product is or how great your advertising is. If you fail to hit the right "bulls-eye" positioning with your webinar… you won't get registrations.

Your title and headline can make or break a webinar!

The Resource Section of this book has a link to plenty of registration page examples for you to peruse. The examples are "frozen in time," so don't be disappointed if the links don't work. Remember: a webinar is a date-driven event.

How to Promote and Generate Leads For Webinars

A webinar is an event with launch components. The biggest obstacle running events is getting people to attend. But before that, the biggest obstacle is getting them to register.

Even before you track registrations, if you do not take the time to analyze where your webinar registrants are coming from it will be hard to replicate your success. Successful webinar presenters do (or someone on the team does). You can track specific social media sites and different banners and post ads on different websites. Facebook, YouTube, and Google Adwords and LinkedIn are great digital choices for advertising. Ideally, you are implementing and utilizing campaign tracking helps drive registrations even higher for future webinars by optimizing your promotion budget and fine-tuning your target demographics.

You webinar headline should tell the story in your first five words. It is an invitation to an event. Anita Campbell has two title formats that work well:

- Help them solve a problem. Example: "How to Survive an I-9 Audit from the INS Without Paying Fines" or "The 7 Things Employers Must Do to Avoid I-9 Fines."
- Entice them with something they desire. Example: "How to Get Traffic to Your Website" or "How I Got 2 Million Monthly Visitors to My Website."

Prospects have a choice to make at every step in the promotion process. At each step there are three choices visitors make (continue, go somewhere else on site, or exit). If your registration page is competing with other demands, such as content on a blog, they may click somewhere else. It is important that the registration page has a single focus. For them to complete that process, we must help them make the right decisions along the way.

Here's an example of a seven-step conversion process:

1. Webinar prospect reads email, Tweet, Facebook post, blog post or advertisement, or watches video
2. Webinar prospect clicks link
3. He lands on webinar registration page with compelling headline and details

4. He clicks to register
5. He enters his email address
6. He clicks on social icon on thank-you page and shares link with other people
7. He checks email for a bonus download link

You want to drive interested people to a registration page that:

- Describes what the webinar is about and the value attendees will receive. (Plan for five to seven bullets or up to two short paragraphs.)
- Offers clear details including date, time, length.
- Identifies presenters just enough to establish credibility.
- Has a prominent call-to-action button

Keep it tight and concise. The longer the registration page, the more people bounce away. You can add more on the thank you page.

Commitment level increases as people move through the process. It starts with zero, or very low, commitment when they arrive at the web page and builds slowly as they begin to enter personal information and move through registration and thank you confirmation pages. Continue to close and sell the smart decision to register with a bonus or information that strengthens their decision to register.

Track and study the webinar invitation, confirmation and reminder email statistics because this will guide you to improve webinar titles, descriptions, timing and registration processes.

We can't continue without discussing advertising campaigns. Both Google Ad Words, Facebook Ads, the Content Display Network are all ready to take your money and show your ads. Ads may become a considerable investment. Test your ads.

Facebook uses ad sets and Gary Henderson and his team created many ad sets for a big launch. The business category is not mentioned. The ad budget that Gary worked on for a client was $25,000 on Facebook for the webinar campaign.

283 ad sets launched

322 total registrations at $3 each

Gary didn't stop there and continued to optimize:

62 ad sets turned off that generated 57 registrations at $7.92 each.

221 ad sets still active that generated 267 registrations at $1.95 each

Spend of about $1956 for 646 registrations. The average is $3.00 each.

Growing your list using ads and getting webinar registrations requires a budget, testing and is an iterative process.

Fortune in the Follow-up with Ad Promotions that can go Viral

Does social proof work? How many times have you clicked on a Facebook ad because it had 100+ comments or likes?

- Turn your webinar recording into an automated replay webinar.
- Create and upload a webinar ad and include the webinar URL into Facebook

- Pin the ad at the top of your social media page(s) i.e. Facebook and Twitter
- At the end of each of your webinar events include your Call To Action (CTA) for your participants to drive your audience to the webinar ad link. Ask them to share the most valuable thing they learned during the webinar or share some positive feedback (This will instantly give you a stream of more comments, likes, the more people sign up for your webinar. particularly for automated webinars.)
- The more viral your webinar ad becomes the more social proof you create which will attract even more people to your event… even if people don't know who you are; this builds your power position.

25 Ways to Promote Your Webinar

Remember WAMO? The M – Message – is also the medium with a webinar. That makes online perfect because the marketing promotion matches the medium. Your marketing message must speak to the needs of your audience. The outcome of your promotion is to get a registration.

Remember the 3Cs – Content, Connection and Close? Your marketing has both Content (copy, graphics, video) that creates Connection and asks for a close. The Close is getting the registration sign-up. With a simple click, your prospect can be signing-up on the registration page.

> **"The most effective promotion is the one that causes a person to take an action because of some internal issue the person tells himself."**

As mentioned, the title of your webinar should summarize why someone should show up to your webinar with the primary "big benefit" clear for visitors.

Test and reuse the winning marketing campaign formula and elements when you have one with great conversion results. Lay out your marketing campaign and follow a process map. Listed below are 25 suggestions for both online and offline promotion opportunities for webinars. Thanks to Bob Hanson for his additions to these 25 suggestions.

Social Media Promotion

1. Facebook – probably the best place to advertise as well as promote in posts on your personal page or business page. Use the SHARE feature found in social media. (Also buy Facebook ads and retargeting ads.) Facebook Live is great inside groups. Also use chatbots inside Facebook Messanger for a texting style more one on one communication.

2. Other Social Media – Promote your webinar and ask for shares. Use an automated service to set up posts with webinar registration links in advance.

> a. Twitter – Promote and advertise your webinar and ask for retweets. Use an auto-tweet service with multiple messages that include webinar information and links.
>
> b. Instagram, LinkedIn, Google+, Other Social Media – There are numerous mini-blogs and social media tools where you can post your webinar information and links. (Also Google ads and LinkedIn ads.)

3. Video – Video is a great tool to tell a story and introduce your webinar. Use free and paid services: YouTube and Vimeo. The right headline and keywords will help people find you and your message about your webinar. Include links on Facebook Live and social media videos to your webinar landing page

Include timed tweets and posts (one hour until, 30 minutes until, starting now…) on the day of the webinar.

Use real-time video such as Facebook Live, Snapchat, and Periscope streaming etc. to capture last minute webinar prospects. Ask for viewers to share the registration link. You could make it into a contest.

Website Page, Registration Page, Thank You Page

4. Website Landing Page – The registration page may include information on what they will learn, what questions they will get answered, what they can expect or experience during the webinar, etc. Small ads and listings drive prospects to the web page, which should have an excellent headline, summary features and benefits, an introductory video, and an easy way to opt-in, which is a great way to convert traffic on your site to webinar registrants and leads. Remember, *capturing* the email address gives you the ability to have a conversation and connect with your prospective customer. The social share buttons (icons) should be prominent on your thank you confirmation page. The one action you want on the registration is getting the email address.

You can also automate interactivity with chat bots on Facebook after interest has been shown by a prospect.

Advertise and Remarket

5. Facebook Advertising – This was already mentioned as part of social media, but it is an important channel and part of the webinar promotion formula. All the social channels have advertising, Twitter, LinkedIn as well as Google and the CPA networks. You need to know how to target custom audiences both via the platform, your website and remarketing on other websites, or you need to work with an ad expert who can handle this for you. You'll need tracking code pixels and retargeting code placed appropriately before you launch your webinar ad campaign. Website visitor data is stored for varying lengths of time: Twitter 90 days. Facebook and Google AdWords 180 days. This gives you additional time to get your message in front of your custom audience.

6. Banner Ads, Content Networks, Related Ads

> (a.) Your own home page or blog– The banner can be placed on the highest traffic pages on your site and direct prospects to your web page, which sells the webinar and asks for a registration.
>
> (b.) Related content sites – Banners can reach new target prospects and drive them to your web page, which has compelling content to sell your webinar and ask for a registration.

7. Solo Ads in Media Ezine Newsletters – Promote using solo ads. Confirm there is no conflict with competitor ads being featured in the same newsletter as your advertisement.

Newsletter Ezines

8. Listings in Relevant Newsletters – Can be low-cost or free because an e-newsletter may be looking for pertinent events and content. This is more commonly used for educational webinars or webinars with outside speakers.

9. Listings on Related Content Sites – Small free or paid ads can pay big dividends in lead generation in general, and webinars could be a great offer to feature.

10. Google Ads – Webinars and webinar archives can be promoted in your paid search ads. Test a webinar offer versus a free report offer. This is considered most often to promote archives of educational webinars.

Email Announcement and Invitations

Use your email list, rent lists, or joint venture with someone else's list of customers.

The subject line of your email about the webinar is to get them to open it. Next, click on the link to the registration page. The registration page must be compelling enough for a sign-up.

Use a reliable email service for deliverability. If it doesn't get delivered, it doesn't get opened.

1. Email subject line (the headline) –The prime benefit of the webinar could also be the subject line used for the email invitation. While one could take an entire course on headline or title writing alone, remember that the subject line of the email is critical because it is your "ad for an ad." This affects your Open Rate.

2. Marketing copy – The purpose of the webinar invitation is to "sell" the webinar, and any information included should compel a visitor to register. Get their attention, spark interest, channel desire, and close by asking for an action (clicking the link in the email). You first get their attention with the subject/headline. Next, create interest within the initial text of your email. This could be questions, a story or example, or a nagging problem they face. An effective way to make sure you generate

their desire is to summarize the case for your webinar in 3 to 7 phrases, sentences, or bullet points, which are almost entirely focused on benefits. Now that your invitation has their attention and builds up interest and desire, take them to the next step: clicking the link. This affects your Click-thru Rate.

3. Details and call-to-action – It depends on your audience, your style—if you give them details in your email or provide a teaser that gets them to click the link. If your customer list expects full details, then describe the webinar: title, timing, speaker or speakers, and any bonuses or extras given as a part of registering or attending the webinar. The invitation also includes whether the webinar is free or has a cost. [Caution: Many webinar announcements focus on background information on the company, speaker, or related products or services. This information often does nothing to focus the reader on the BENEFITS of the webinar. Minimize or avoid this in the invitation process.] This affects your Conversion Rate—the registration sign-up!

11. Email Invitations – Your List – The most common way of inviting prospects to a webinar. Make sure to link to a dedicated registration form. For most businesses, this is the primary way of drawing an audience to their webinars.

12. Email Invitations – Rented List – Only rent lists with verified opt-in names. The price of the rental typically includes design and mailing costs. Response rates can vary widely, from negligible to as much as 4 percent or more.

13. Emails from JV Partners or Guest Speakers – Many times, with joint events, your speakers will mail to their customer list as well. This is a way to add to your own list. Use your compelling invitation copy to maximize response.

14. Endorsed Emails from Third-Party Organizations – Third-party organizations can be sponsors or equal partners in your webinar. Send emails to their list of customers with your copy coming from someone in their organization whom the target market knows and trusts. This email can be even more responsive than your list. A great offer to an endorsed list can be one of your most successful marketing campaigns.

15. Repeat Successful Messages – If something works, consider repeating it before the event. For example: if an email or banner ad invitation pulls more registrations, then send a "Last Chance" email 24 or 48 hours before the event. Also, use successful tactics for future events. In all emails, ask prospects or customers to "Forward Your Webinar Invitation."

Alternative Promotion

16. Press Release/Free Media – Assuming your webinar is newsworthy, or built for coverage such as a channel or product launch, you may get a mention of your webinar in certain media. As a potential promotional outlet, consider upcoming event calendars which often promote live events. Press Releases are highly recommended.

17. SMS Text – Use this primarily as a reminder, on the day of the webinar, by sending a text message with details. This may be part of your webinar platform or may be an additional software service.

18. Fax or Voice Broadcast to Your Own List – Typically these are used to target a better segment of your own list, such as your customers. Sometimes they are used for events where you are targeting hard to reach decision makers.

Direct Mail and Other Media Promotion

If your webinar is planned for some point in the future or is an automated webinar where your prospect can select a date and time, direct mail is a great avenue. You can use SRDS and NextMark to rent marketing lists.

19. Direct Mail Invitations – Using multi-component mailing, with an invitation letter and a response card, is more typically found in live seminar marketing campaigns, but it's a proven way of recruiting your audience.

20. Direct Mail Postcards – Use print invitation copy that aligns with your email invitation and put it on a two-sided postcard. Direct mail postcards could be part of any lead generation program, and webinars make a great offer for this marketing vehicle.

21. Free Standing Insert – A postcard-size card or leaflet inserted in a newspaper or magazine. Free standing inserts can be cheaper and more effective than either direct mail or advertising in the media itself.

Telephone Promotion

22. Telemarketing – This technique is especially effective if you are promoting a paid webinar. You can use your own telemarketing team or an outside firm. Typically telemarketing is best done in combination with other media, like email or direct mail invitations.

23. Sales Calls (Lead script or second option) – Webinar invitations can be a good opener for salespeople to use in their outbound calling, especially to relatively cool or cold lists. They also act as a fallback if the primary sales pitch fails to gain interest. It provides a way of getting groups of email addresses and adding them to a list.

Promoting At Other Events

24. Discuss Upcoming Webinars at a Trade Show or Live Seminar or on the Next Webinar – Especially if you are running a webinar series with a theme, you can discuss your upcoming webinar in the introduction and as a reminder at the end of the event.

25. Hand Out One-Page Announcements for Webinars (at live events, trade shows and in-person seminars) – This is particularly good for perpetual-automated webinars. Add one or two free gifts as an incentive. Give one with registration and indicate that they will receive another bonus when they attend the webinar.

TESTING: Advertising

Brian Bagnall uses Facebook ads to drive people to live and automated webinars. Test your advertising, test your registration landing page, and test your webinar to find the sweet spot on price and what the hot buttons are to buy from you.

Brian Bagnall is also a big fan of webinars. Listen to his interview on webinars for some very smart tips.

Lewis Howes says the cost of his Facebook ads usually works out to a dollar a lead. If you're promoting an offer that sells, you often make your money back and keep the leads for free.

Listen to *The Webinar Way* interview with Crystal Curtis. She uses our webinar promotion formula, which is a simple four-part formula plus your auto-responder. It includes 1) a paid Facebook ad with a catchy headline that takes you to 2) a free Facebook page with an expanded headline that includes 3) a registration form and a 4) YouTube video as part of her Facebook landing page. The custom landing page is actually a tab on her Facebook page, which brings in the webinar registration page format. These parts, together, all promote her webinar.

Marketing expert Frank Kern says that an acceptable opt-in rate (providing name and email) for webinar registrations from cold traffic is 20%. As mentioned earlier, live show-up rates for your webinar are from 3% to 60% (rare).

Let's say you have a product that sells for $500. You plan on doing one live webinar a month. If you start advertising and promoting 30 days in advance of your webinar and get about 50 visitors a day with a Facebook ad that you pay $1 per click for, then:

- 1500 visitors to the registration page (Cost $1500)
- 300 registrants (20% opt-in rate)
- 180 attendees (60% show rate)

A webinar that converts at a mere 5% is decent, and most are higher. To break even on your advertising costs in our example above, your webinar needs to convert at a very reasonable 2%, which is 3 sales. Then more sales come in from the replay. You can test the price and set-up an automated webinar for more sales conversions.

There are a lot of elements of advertising cost—everything from your audience to your bidding plan to ranking directly affects and influences how much you're going to pay. Keep in mind that what you spend on advertising is up to you and how you set your budget.

Also, you have to decide if you will also advertise on mobile. Then you need to customize ads for mobile delivery.

Most advertising works like an auction. You say how much you are willing to pay for an ad, otherwise it will be automatically calculated for you. You are entering a bid for eyeballs. The audience you're targeting, the quality of your ad, the time of year (holidays) and other factors affect your ad price.

While looking at ad cost and ad spending is important, what's even more important is the CPA (cost per action) and the ROI (return on investment) you're getting. This is how you can determine whether what you're paying—and what your ad is costing you—is worth it. Does your ROI have a higher value than your CPA?

Your landing page and offer (lead candy) play huge factors in actually getting conversions, and this is how they'll affect the cost of your ads.

Ann Gotter says there are different types of bidding options, or ways you can pay for Facebook ads. These include:

Cost per click (CPC): You are paying only for each user that clicks on your ad. They do not have to complete the conversion and purchase on your site or sign up on your landing page; they just have to click. That being said, you aren't paying for users who viewed your ad and didn't convert.

- Impressions (CPM): You're paying for cost per 1,000 impressions. The cost per impressions is much lower than a cost per click, and when you want to get a lot of eyes on your ad, this can be a good way to go. (Note: cost per thousand impressions (CPM), is a term for cost per mille, with the M for 'mille' being Latin for thousand.)

- Cost per action/conversion (CPA): You're paying and bidding on a specific action being taken. This is where you pay for that conversion. These conversions may cost more than clicks, but this bidding option is designed to get you more conversions, providing a much higher ROI.
- Cost per like (CPL): Used in campaigns where the objective is to gain likes on your Page, this will allow you to pay for each like you get from your ad. If you are capturing email addresses it is your Cost per Lead.

Facebook also offers different optimization options, each of which will optimize the ad delivery for users who are likely to take the requested action. These include:

Conversions: Facebook will deliver your ad to people who are most likely to complete the designated action you've chosen (such as purchasing from your site). They evaluate this based on past user history. With this option, you're paying for impressions (CPM).

- Impressions: Facebook will deliver your ad to as many people as possible, getting as many views on your ad that they can. You're paying for impressions (CPM).
- Clicks on your ad/to your site: Facebook will deliver your ad to the people who are most likely to click over to your site. You're paying for cost per click, or CPC.
- Daily Unique Reach: Facebook focuses on delivering your ads to people up to once a day, affecting frequency. You're paying for impressions (CPM).

Facebook will automatically choose a bidding option based on your objective.

There are plenty of webinars, videos, and blog posts on Facebook and Google ad optimization. It is that big of a deal.

PROMOTION: Email, Mobile and Video Reminders

There are several schools of thought on email reminders. Some people have a sequence of 5-7 reminders, including the day of the webinar event: 2-4 hours before the webinar, 30 minutes before the webinar, and 3 minutes after the start of the webinar. You must send several reminders the day of the webinar event. It may take seeing three to five reminders in the hours leading up to the webinar to get registrations and have attendees show up.

If you have mobile reminders from Call Loop software, or the built-in SMS system in the webinar platform, or if you use any other SMS system to send reminders you will get higher attendance.

Your target audience should be exposed to the registration page link multiple times from the time you announce the webinar until the time you are live.

You can use Facebook Live video to hit the news stream at the right time or a custom audience Facebook video ad for folks who have visited your website.

PROMOTION: Content Post-Webinar

> ***"The fortune is in the follow-up."***
>
> *-Jim Rohn*

Perry Marshall says email is a profitable skill that every marketer should master. Listen to the interview with Perry's business partner, Matt Gillogly. His approach to webinars is simple and effective for closing business.

Use email to follow-up the same day with a content summary, and the following days with replay links, content teasers, content benefits, testimonials from participants, testimonials from buyers, etc.

- Stay in the mind's eye of your customer and prospect.
- Use social media to promote the replay on Twitter and Facebook.
- Create a scarcity warning that the there is less than 24 hours to watch the replay.
- Create a good-looking landing page for the replay.
- Have well-timed buy buttons.
- Offer bonuses.
- Include share buttons for Twitter, Facebook, Google+, LinkedIn and other social networks.
- Offer a condensed transcript of the webinar with calls to action.

Once your live webinar has been "perfected" for optimal conversions, you can put it into an automated webinar system. We'll talk about that in the Perpetual Profits section in Part IV of this book.

PILLAR 4: PRESENT

> ***"No argument in the world can ever compare with one dramatic demonstration."***
>
> *- Claude Hopkins,*
> *the father of modern direct response advertising*

Presentation, Presenters, Practice, Participants

- **Presentation:** What do you put in a webinar presentation?
- **Presenters:** How a webinar presenter can make or break the success of a webinar?
- **Practice:** Why does "practice make profit" with webinars?

- **Participants:** How do you turn a passive attendee into an active participant?

Mastering the art of producing effective webinars presentations will give you a definite edge over the competition. You can also repurpose your webinars and monetize them without having to recreate them every time. The right balance of technology, people and processes will enable you to create successful webinars consistently.

It will serve you well if you make webinars a deliberate strategy in your business. Dan Kennedy was aware of this and became a serious student of the architecture, engineering, craftsmanship, and writing of effective presentations that can be transformed into winning webinars. Become competent at webinars, as Dan says, Competence Creates Confidence."

Bond Halbert, son of the great copywriter Gary Halbert, knows a thing or two about the key issue of your prospect. Nestled in your content must be a pre-existing condition. Now, this may sound like something you must reveal to your doctor but in fact, it is your marketing gold. Do you know what your audience issues are?

We get into this in detail in the Power of Webinars training program but for now, make a list. What does your target market fear, what are they angry or frustrated about, what keeps them up at night? How about their wants, desires, and aspirations? What are the trends that are happening that will affect them personally and professionally?

In a live seminar, as well as in a webinar presentation, similar factors impact the tipping point or threshold for the participant to act. The action is the outcome you desire. This participant action is affected by several factors.

3 Core Elements: Content, Connection, Close

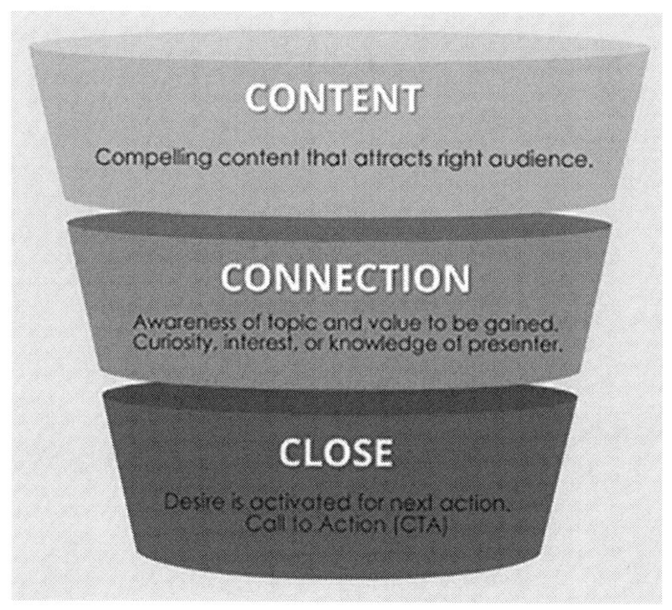

Figure 6

The 3 Core Elements of Content, Connection and Close are now expanded with more detail:

- **Content –** Information, Story, Messages
- **Content –** Visual, Slides, Video, Demos
- **Connection –** Interactivity & Audience Engagement
- **Connection & Close –** Social Proof
- **Close & Convert –** Urgency & Scarcity

Content – Information, Story, Messages

The core content must be relevant and of high perceived value. The presentation content affects the credibility of the presentation. There must be something unique about the content, or in the way it is presented. The storyline connects the participant to the presenter, and the messages are woven throughout the presentation. Include at least one "shock and awe" visual or story to keep the audience on the edge of their seat.

Statistics show that 63% of business marketers at small and mid-sized companies rate webinars as effective content marketing tools *(Content Marketing Institute, B2B Content Marketing 2014).*

Content – Visual, Slides, Video, Demos

The look and feel of your content must be visually stimulating and engage the senses. The visual content is highly influential on your participants. Incorporating rich media and visual aids into your slides make them more interesting and more fun. It can be very time-consuming and also fun to select the right images for your presentation. You want to captivate your audience with great visuals.

Some folks run a workshop on-camera, teaching and answering questions without slides. Not recommended.

However, your slide deck presentation is NOT your webinar. It is a visual aid that enhances what you are teaching. If someone can look at your slide deck and read word for word to get the same training, you're running your webinar the wrong way.

B2B marketers say product demos are the most effective method for lead marketing, followed by educational webinars *(BtoB magazine, Lead Generation: Optimum Techniques for Managing Lead-Gen Campaigns, Nov 2013).*

Connection – Interactivity & Engagement

Deliver an engaging presentation in which attendees actively participate instead of passively watching and listening. Grabbing their attention and holding it during the entire presentation is a challenge because of other available distractions. A contest or prize may force attention. The webinar medium is the perfect interactive tool, so take advantage of the interactivity. Do not deliver one-way, monotonous, boring presentations. Your event instantly becomes more effective if you can turn your attendees into participants. It is possible (and easy) to offer an interactive session while still controlling the flow and not losing control over your webinar event. Keep the participants muted because allowing people to ask questions, verbally on the phone or via their computers (since it is tough to manage a large crowd), can add unexpected echoes or background noises, especially if you are recording the webinar. Interactivity is probably the most critical component in your quest for participant action.

If you wish to grab and hold the attention of your participants, you need to have them take an action every seven minutes. Action may include raising hands, answering questions, taking a poll, taking notes ("write this down"), repeating a phrase after you, etc. In a web-based environment, you face major obstacles and you are competing with so many distractions, such as checking emails, online chatting, Facebook, YouTube movies, interruptions and possibly kids playing or dogs barking in the background.

There are built-in attention detectors with most webinar platforms. The status bars shows if the participant's attentiveness and interest levels.

Use polls to get people to relate to the content and keep them engaged. Refresh the survey data and use Q&A sessions or chat for this too. Know if you are chatting with all participants or to one person. Keep chat open in front of you, or have a moderator do it.

The entire point of a live webinar is to interact with the wonderful participants and allow involvement. Webinars offer all kinds of ways for the audience to interact with your content. At least every seven minutes acknowledge your audience and allow them to participate in some way on the webinar.

Master The Art Of Virtual Interaction

Even though you can't see all your webinar attendees' faces, that doesn't mean you can't see their interaction or engagement level. One of the best presenters is Taki Moore who grabs the attention of a participant and holds everyone in rapt attention for 60-90 minutes. Taki uses 'Attract, Convert, Deliver' as his coaching model. Applying this to the 7 Pillars of the Webinar Way, in zones, and adding Prepare, here is how they match up.

ZONE	WEBINAR WAY PILLAR
Prepare	**Perspective**
	Plan
Attract	**Promote**
	Partner
Deliver	**Present**
	Power Position
Convert	**Pitch**

Present your content to get progressive buy-in. The right order helps participants accept that your offer is right for them.

Taki Moore suggests answering three core questions:

1. Why is this important to me right now? (Issue)
2. What is this all about? (Outcome)
3. How do I get involved? (Solution)

ISSUE	Problem
	Prescription
OUTCOME	Outcome
	Model
SOLUTION	Logistics
	Price

ISSUE

1. Problem – Describes the reason you created your program. "*I saw that many people were being held back by [X,Y,Z].*"
2. Prescription – Briefly describes what prospects need to do to overcome these struggles. "*The first three things you'll want to fix are [A,B,C].*"

OUTCOME

1. Outcome – Describes the results program/course or offer. "*This program will free up 15 hours a week, add 90 lbs to your bench-press, double your income, or allow you to present one-to-many to increase conversions.*"

2. Model – Visually represents the content. A simple graphic that sums up what your program focuses on. *In my program, Power of Webinars, we focus on three areas: How to* ***invite*** *the right audience, How to* ***delight*** *those prospects while combining teaching and selling, so that we can* ***deliver*** *a great experience and results while turning prospects into clients.*

Figure 7

SOLUTION

1. Logistics – Describe how the program works. "*We meet twice a month through webinars, share in our group, review assignments…*"
2. Price – Tell them how much the program costs and reinforce the value it will bring them.

By using this progression, a prospect easily decides to become a client. A smart webinar presenter wouldn't start the offer by talking about price because this creates a barrier in participant's mind before you demonstrate the value they'll receive. Instead, start by telling them why it matters (issues), then move on to what's involved (outcome), and end by showing them how it works (solution).

Instead of housekeeping at the onset of your webinar, set expectations. Give rules. Dave VanHoose uses these four rules: 1) Have fun 2) I promise to give 100 percent 3) This is interactive, so the more you give me, the more I give you, and 4) You'll take action. The four rules are designed to get attendees to say, YES, so that when you present your offer, the participants take action.

Here are few ways to make your webinar event more engaging:

- Before the start of the actual presentation, ask casual questions, as you want to create a friendly environment. As part of the webinar welcome, ask early audience members to enter their first name in the Q&A and then welcome a few of the attendees by name. You can also ask what city or country they are from because this builds rapport right at the start. Use first names if you are using a moderated Q&A where participants cannot see submitted questions– this lets them know they are not alone and you recognize their presence and question..

- Use the Q&A/Chat in the webinar room before the start of the webinar. Have an ice-breaker question or post a link to a download. You can post the same question or link more than once as eyes notice the activity on the screen. These questions can help set the tone and lets the participants know they are not alone.
- Get to the content FAST! ***Give Them the Content They Crave!***
- During the webinar session, ask people to comment or ask questions via chat, and make sure you or the moderator answer most questions. Providing answers allows participants to make an educated decision and brings them closer to taking action.
- Take frequent polls and, depending on the question, share the results with the attendees.
- BONUS – You may include bonuses for showing up. Digital bonuses that can be downloaded are the easiest. You may include a “fill in the blanks” document to print and follow along.
- You might want to ask them to play a game on the webinar platform. Some web platforms allow you to start quiz games.
- Have at least two presenters or speakers. Experiencing dialogs, instead of monologs, is more engaging.
- Include the link to a web page in the chat (towards the end of your pitch) where they can take action such as registering for a service or purchasing a product. Some

web conference platforms also incorporate shopping carts.

- Get feedback. Depending on your desired outcome, when you end the webinar, take attendees to a survey page or send a thank you email that includes a survey link.

Depending on your webinar platform and other features, using annotation tools for pointing, writing, and highlighting can provide movement and attract eyeballs.

Another key to your connection and interaction is to keep the proper pace. Start out with a killer introduction and great visuals and set the tone for the rest of the webinar. Be ready to deliver on the promises of the webinar invitation. Pace yourself so you don't rush through the essential information later in your presentation.

Connection & Close – Social Proof

Robert Cialdini has written extensively about Social Proof in his book *Influence: The Psychology of Persuasion*. In the chapter on Social Proof, he suggests that "one means we use to determine what is correct is to find out what other people think is correct… We view a behavior as more correct in a given situation to the degree that we see others performing it." Social Proof is the premise that people's behavioral patterns are highly influenced by the actions of the people or community around them. In a webinar, it is powerful to show results of customers, have a current customer share their experience and identify, by name, people who have asked relevant questions, purchased or taken action on the webinar.

There are a few different ways to communicate to your participants and have them take an action since others are doing it. For example:

- Show them the list of attendees, or at least past attendees
- Show them intense participation using interactive chat
- Display the number of products sold and write on a slide "only X left," as part of a countdown
- Play testimonial movies or, for even more effectiveness, have a satisfied customer talk live. If you are doing a software demo, invite one person, a prospect, to join and un-mute them. Ask them, with specific questions, what they think of the software.

There is a snowball effect when you master the art of social proof. On a live webinar, showing real-time social proof is compelling. It is more powerful than the testimonials posted on your website.

Eben Pagan held several webinars, as a last minute push, as part of his product launch. There were less than ten slides and there was no demo. These webinars were in fact teleseminars using webinar technology to deliver. Webinars have higher perceived value than a teleseminar. The point is that the reason the webinar was effective was that Eben had multiple guests, who were former students, describe where they were when they started (their pain point) and where they are now (their gain point), which demonstrated success. The webinar participants asked questions and the social proof was outstanding.

Close & Convert – Urgency & Scarcity

There is empirical proof that timing is critical to a sale or a next action, and potential customers are more likely to purchase at the time when exposed to time-sensitive offers. Therefore, the sense of urgency at the close of your webinar is to get your participants to act as fast as possible to get bonuses or special limited quantity discounts. The sense of urgency, coupled with social proof, is powerful.

How you deliver your powerful close will affect your sales outcome. You want participants to feel this is an irresistible offer they must buy now. Leveraging the real-time deadline with urgency is tremendously effective. You can present time-sensitive offers during the webinar. You may show a countdown timer and set a discount or special offer for a limited time or webinar-only price. Urgency and social proof are particularly useful in live webinar environments.

STORY and STORYBOARDING

The basis of a presentation is about the most ancient of social rituals: storytelling. It's telling the story differently, more engagingly, in a way that draws the participants in, making their eyes open a little wider and their jaws drop ever so slightly. Make it showware (show + webinar software) by combining movie script features plus education and demos. And as they process it, it can sometimes change their perspective altogether and possibly open their digital wallets to buy what you, the webinar storyteller, are offering.

You can use software such as mind mapping or flow chart software as your storyboard—your webinar "show." You can brainstorm your story using a Persuasion Map to map out your ideas. You can also use index cards, sticky notes or note cards to storyboard your webinar. Find or create supporting quotes, facts, graphics, and images. Images and graphics support your story. Inside PowerPoint (or some other presentation software), use the slide sorter view to look at your presentation in a storyboard format.

Build a "*F.A.M.E. Example*" into your presentation. As part of your storyboarding exercise, incorporate your *F.A.M.E.* = * *Fascination* * *Achieves* * *Memorable* * *Experiences*

Include the appropriate *F.A.M.E. Examples* such as a dramatic demonstration, memorable sound bites, visuals that evoke emotion, shocking statistics, and an awe-inspiring story. Make it memorable and fascinate your audience. Visuals, shocking statistics, and the text of your sound bite should be on a stand-alone single slide for most significant impact.

According to Carmen Simon, you can influence memory. The 15 variables that influence memory are: context, cues, distinctiveness, emotion, facts, familiarity, motivation, novelty, surprise, relevance, repetition, sensory intensity, the quantity of information, self-generated content, and social aspects. The key is knowing using both logic and creativity which variables to employ, how much to use them, and when to use them.

People take action on what they remember so make your webinar core teaching points memorable!

The expression 15 minutes of fame coined by Andy Warhol who said, in 1968, "In the future, everyone will be world-famous for 15 minutes." That was before the Internet. You don't need 15 minutes now for a well-remembered *F.A.M.E. Example* that can become a viral phenomenon. On your webinar, make it easy for people to share their favorite *F.A.M.E. Example* from your webinar and ASK them to do it. People respond to requests such as to a tweet on Twitter or a share on Facebook.

Start with a Killer Hook! If you are using a slide deck, your first slide is critical, so use an evocative visual or shocking statistic. This bears repeating. Your first slide is vital to grab attention. If you are streaming live, make your PROMISE at the beginning of the presentation. Have this well-rehearsed. What they are going to discover goes first. Let webinar attendees get oriented when they enter the webinar event, and seeing the first slide with the promise lets them know they are in the right place while waiting for the webinar to begin.

Incorporate how you would engage your audience in a live environment into your webinar presentation. Plan to engage your audience and practice asking questions, conducting polls, responding to questions. You're bringing them on this journey with you, so keep people engaged and interacting with you. If you think of the journey as a road with a clear destination, keep your participants on *The Webinar Way* and don't let them veer off onto Distraction Avenue. They won't get distracted and multi-task if you are interesting, fascinating, and able to keep their attention. Weave in who you are, your credentials and your story throughout the presentation, whether you are using slides, streaming video or demonstration.

PRESENTATION SOFTWARE PROGRAMS

There are four areas of major decisions to make for your webinar. We mentioned two already, deciding on a webinar software platform and how you will promote. The other two decisions are around your presentation. How will you come across with your human elements: voice/audio only or face/live-stream? The other is the type of presentation you will be running: slideshow, demo, with or without handouts, worksheets, etc.

There are several choices to build your presentation if you are using slides. Microsoft PowerPoint and Apple Keynote are the two most popular, followed by Prezi and SlideRocket. These may be included with your computer, and if not they are available for purchase. The free options are OpenOffice and Google Slides. Google Slides are excellent for collaborative slide deck creation.

TIP: Using PowerPoint – Enter into the theater mode to expand to the entire desktop. Be sure to first set your monitor's resolution to the highest possible setting.

- Tip1: make sure the start menu bar is set to auto-hide for better appearance
- Tip2: click to slide 2 and then back to slide 1 before the webinar starts—this will eliminate the PowerPoint navigation overlay

Have a look at a great example of Prezi on *The Webinar Way* YouTube Channel. Use motion graphics in your webinar to provide better value and share your story in a visually stunning way. There are several links for presentation examples and videos in the Resource Section.

Use these elements to enhance your webinar presentation:

- **Size (text, graphics)**
- **Color**
- **Orientation**
- **Motion (flicker) animation, movement, zooming, text size expansion**
- **Photos and images**

Check out the video listed in the Resource Section called "Share Message" that illustrates these elements.

Test your font size by reducing your whole presentation to 50%. If you can't read it at a glance, the fonts are too small.

Webinar design is about deciding which patterns and elements to focus on, building a narrative, and telling the story with visual images, data, visuals and anecdotes that you present in a unique and compelling way.

Your information is only as good as your ability to share it in a way that has an emotional impact. Get the B-spot activated! We'll talk more about the B-spot (brain-mind-emotions) in Presentation Practice in a few pages.

Your target audience, your subject and your style will determine the content of your presentation content. Here's a sequence you can adapt for your own use:

Simple Presentation Sequence

The webinar tells a story. If you think of a TV program, it starts with the hook in the first few minutes with no commercials or interruptions. Then there is the opening credit sequence, with the show title and star names, which takes place quickly (about a minute), and then the story continues.

- Pre-webinar chatter: Ask for social sharing (Facebook, Twitter)
- Big Hook on first slide displayed during Introduction & Welcome (2-4 minutes)
- Optional: Introduce stay-to-end bonus or contest
- What this is about, who this is for, who this is NOT for, any catches (1-2 minutes)
- Connect: Weave in *"Your Story"* (throughout)
- State problem/pain points, spotlight the gap getting to the gain point (5-10 minutes). Teach.
- Connect: *"Do You See Yourself"* style questions for rapport (several times). Apply.
- Promise to bridge the gap and solve their problem
- Connect: Engage and interact (several times). Pre-sell.
- Expose more of the problem and pain (3-5 minutes)
- Teach an action they can do now, by themselves (4-5 minutes). Apply.
- Share a better way and build the benefits (10-15 minutes)
- Provide proof or case studies (5-15 minutes). Stories.
- More compelling content (10-20 minutes). Teach.
- More actions they can do now, by themselves. Apply.
- Dialog: (optional) un-mute participant or client. Pre-sell.

- Close with the offer (10-15 minutes). Sell.
- Describe your guarantee (as part of the close)
- Optional Q&A (5 minutes to hours)

Start your webinar by creating a connection with your participants, not just teaching or giving content. Be upfront with what participants will learn and be transparent so they know what's going to happen and what you will be doing. The connect aspect of your webinar builds rapport and engagement. There are many different ways to begin your webinar; here are a few ideas:

1. Ask people where they are from – and make them feel at home.

2. Greet as many of your attendees as possible by "first name" as the webinar starts.

3. Engage the audience with questions/interaction (set the expectation by telling them that you heard that they are a smart group; ask questions and foster participation).

4. Ask them to share something specific on Twitter or Facebook and include a hashtag to build a community (i.e. #webinarway).

5. Optional: Incentivize attendees to stay until the end by announcing that you'll give out something "Special," "Exclusive" or "Rare" in the close of the webinar.

6. Address technical questions/complaints (verbally, not just in the chat/questions box) about the webinar platform, audio, etc. Or address technical questions in a video with the registration sequence.

Visual content is critical especially during the first few slides. If you are using streaming video, have a strong, powerful initial statement. Make sure your presentation looks great, because your audience will be watching for 60-120 minutes. Only touch upon your story at the beginning and teach something of value right away. Share or teach something that can be applied to the participants' situation early in your webinar.

Research an industry trade organization that can give you significant facts, graphs, charts and statistics about your product, or any studies made that provide facts and figures that will substantiate your claims. Use a hard-hitting statistic to jolt the audience awake, but limit the number of statistics at the beginning of the presentation. Spotlight the "gap" of where they are and where they want to be, because this is how you can aggravate the problem and identify yourself as the one with the solution.

Listen to *The Webinar Way* interview with Dolan Ramsay Gadoury about presentations. He was kind enough to share a detailed presentation sequence outline that you can download and modify for your use. There is no one-size-fits-all presentation format for webinars.

Just a reminder that a webinar you build with the intention of selling or getting a specific action has a different format than a pure teaching webinar. Use webinars for each stage of the customer journey by changing the intent of the content as your customer's questions, goals and needs change.

Online learning is increasingly a way to keep your skills up to date and learn entirely new skills. There are many advocates of the power of online learning and webinars are the right vehicle.

Forbes Magazine reported in 2015 that the online learning industry is poised for $107 billion and it is growing each year. In the 21st century, teaching sells.

Presentation Design Tips

Simple sentences distill an idea into a short and sweet sound bite. These one-liners make good memorable slides with the right image. Use one concept per slide, with perhaps a recap.

Don't use slides filled with text and bullet points. Too much text is read faster than spoken. Keep slides slim not jam-packed or too dense. People get bored and tune out and start traveling down Distraction Avenue instead of staying on Webinar Way.

Use a similar format for text on one slide. Check your tense agreement. Use numbers to track ideas. Show single questions on a slide. Create simple visual slides that can show body language to highlight your point.

If you use graphs, ask yourself if they can be understood at a glance. If not, drop any unnecessary details.

Think mini info-graphics for your slides. Use auto-shapes in PowerPoint to create the feeling of motion, outline a sequence, and find parent-child (like persuasion map) relationships. Auto-shapes give words a visual component.

The shapes give your framework life. Use circles, squares, triangles, rectangles, arrows, icebergs, pyramids, dials, Venn diagrams, quadrant/matrix, and puzzle pieces. Depending on your subject and audience, you can use emoticons.

There is a specific and unique way to set up your slides that incorporates how the each of the elements relates to one another within a group of ideas. There are outstanding points that can and should be repeated at the appropriate time.

Expressive shapes and lightning bolts carry impact. Stars, speech bubbles, thought cloud, and comic cartoons can add meaning when used wisely. Use SIZE for emphasis.

Figure 8

Avoid clipart if possible. Photos and images are best. Be kind to the eyes. Pictures enhance your words. The same photo with a different caption or overlay text has a different meaning. Images should support the story you are telling and enhance the point. Images should be memorable.

In photos, heads and eyes should face into the slide, not looking outward (unless that is the emotion you want to evoke). Our eyes tend to look where the eyes are looking.

Colors should be in sync unless you change the color for dramatic effect. Don't make slides look like a 1960s psychedelic trip—that will make your participants dizzy.

Use animations sparingly. As a substitute for animations, create a directional relationship with arrows, adding images to build or grow, and to create movement. Test it all on your webinar platform during the practice run.

For emphasis, use quotes and images from iconic people because this can inspire confidence and trust if the icon is synonymous with certain situations or desired outcomes.

Your participants will derive meaning from the way you organize your presentation. You and your offer will be perceived by verbal and visual cues you present and these cues are then filtered through your participants' own memories, values, meanings, beliefs, and expectations.

For recaps, or when switching from presentation to demo and back to the presentation, create transitions slides to give the feeling of "but wait, there's more…"

If you have a closing Q&A slide, include the Offer link or Take Action link on the slide.

Write, edit, choose images, practice, refine, switch images and practice your webinar presentation multiple times. Work with a webinar coach to refine your presentation.

Know What to Emphasize

Emphasis. The aural reception enhances the visual presentation. Your presenter notes or script help keep you on track. Steve Trister, trained comedian and the creator of the *Professional Presenter Blueprint,* suggests color-coding your script for emphasis, as well as adding bold and italic text as part of your practice. There is no color coding in the example below, but the "/" is used for a brief pause for effect.

Here's the thing./ Once you've **bought** the program and **put this stuff into practice**, **I'll** be the one / that everyone talks about/… for being **so charismatic**, / totally engaging, / funny, / entertaining, and real./ Your audience / is going to remember you / for *who you are* / and/ what you stand for. / They **won't shut up about you.**

Listen to Steve's interview on *The Webinar Way*. It is a unique interview because it was done right after his first practice webinar with a small group of participants. That only happens once in a lifetime. Even though he is an experienced live presenter on stage, the new environment of a webinar took some getting used to, even though he had practiced solo many times.

We've discussed the idea of a movie storyboard to plan your presentation. Choose your cast and crew carefully to support your success. Your cast is performing and they definitely must rehearse. Utilize a mentor the way a director guides an actor on where to put the emphasis.

Choose your words wisely, and practice the key phrases and the sound bites that you want to be memorable for your audience.

Webinars have *reached* the tipping point.

Webinars have reached the *tipping point.*

Accentuate keywords and repeat a phrase to drive home the point and prepare for a transition. The example below would transition to a slide with a graph or chart.

Webinars have *reached* the tipping point. Webinars have reached the *tipping point* **because** the survey facts are in… While less than 1% stated they could call themselves a webinar master, over 35% say they have presented on a webinar, and over 60% of people have attended a webinar. There are fewer people now who have never attended a webinar.

PRESENTERS

You don't have to be alone on your pilot webinar presentation. You may have a co-host.

Working with other presenters is like dating. You need to get to know each other.

Prepare Your Guest Presenter

- **Set Expectations**. Your guest presenter might be accustomed to being on webinars, but no two webinars are run the same. Be clear on the webinar schedule. For any webinar, and particularly for webinar-based online summits, this is a good Day-of webinar schedule:

  30 min before the scheduled start time: Host and guest start testing audio levels and software

  Start time to 5 min: Welcomes, expectations/housekeeping and intros

  Content portion: Guest takes over for presentation, invitation to call to action

  Final section: Questions from participants, wrap-up, invitation to call to action (again)

- **Make it a Power Deck.** Don't just expect that their slide deck will be great - give help. You can prepare slide templates in Power Deck style for your guest presenter in their preferred format (such as Keynote or PowerPoint) in advance. Once they're done adding their content and offer (CTA invitation) they send it back to you to review. This review gives you a chance to provide valuable feedback and fix any errors.

- **Your Practice is a Dress Rehearsal**. With more people, you absolutely need to practice. Think of it as a tutorial. Get a handle on the moving parts with screen sharing software, broadcasting capabilities, and the slide presentation. Each additional presenter has their own assumptions, habits, script, knowledge of webinar platform (or lack tech know-how) and agenda. Lessen any technical hiccups by doing a practice dry-run a week before the webinar go-live date. Use the same technology: webinar platform and computer hardware (audio headset). Wireless is not recommended for computer or phone. A hard-wired Internet connection is best. It also really helps to get a third person (or even third computer signed in as an attendee) to join the practice run as an attendee to check that there are no audio or video troubles and your transitions are smooth.

The number of presenters on a webinar may vary. There are pros and cons to all and the level of interactivity and logistics is different between them. Here are a few examples:

- Solo-Presenter
- Two Presenters – same subject matter (guest presenter)
- Interview Style – often used in JV presentations with clearly defined question points
- Panel Discussion – with moderator
- Fully Interactive Training Webinar – all "lines" open

- Webinar Summit – one-day or better as multi-day with hosts and multiple presenters and panels. (This is also in the category of a Joint Venture Summit.) Summits are a huge time investment.

Set a "date" to plan your webinar event agenda. If you have Webinar Promoter (JV Broker) in the mix then they usually coordinate the date for the "meet and greet."

Prior to your webinar, hold a "meet and greet" with the other presenters using Skype, Zoom or conference call. Ask presenters to send a photograph and brief biographical description that you can use for registration and intro slides. Identify and handle other logistics. Determine what questions will be asked and the order in which the speakers will present. Coordinate to run through the presentation to understand the speaker transitions, if this is a shared presentation. If this is a hosted presentation, determine if there are appropriate spots for the host to ask questions and create participant engagement and interaction. Get to know the tools built into your webinar platform and practice together to help keep you going in the right direction.

Also, before the webinar, probably on the practice rehearsal, check that all presenters, hosts and moderators can 'find' the location. Locate the email with their login details during the practice run, and overcome issues related to browsers, or any technical concerns.

One great presentation can make you rich. But an in-person physical presentation is different from a webinar presentation. Adjust accordingly. If you are transitioning as an experienced speaker from live stage presentations to virtual environments, and starting out as a new webinar presenter for the first time via online delivery, give careful thought and preparation to the transition.

Start on time on your webinar day. Have the webinar room "open" with a killer slide at least 15 minutes before the webinar is supposed to start. (This webinar room is sometimes called the lobby) Be ready. Prepare to impress. Remember: this is an event and you will be judged on your execution and delivery.

If you have a co-host, they can read a short bio about you. If you are presenting alone, weave your story and credentials into the presentation.

Include in your welcome script that the webinar will be interactive and that the participants' questions will be answered. Show them how it works early on in the presentation. Answer an audience-given question early on.

Have the host ask the audience to "grab a pen and get ready to take some notes."

Have the host do a show and tell them about the webinar platform, and give specific instructions where the tools can be found. You can even include a slide with a few arrows pointing out the key features of the webinar platform.

Have the host verbally cue the participants that you are going to start a poll. Don't expect 100% participation. At about 70-80% you can share the poll. Verbally tell them you are going to close the poll.

Your comfort level with your co-host and the feeling of genuine connection between the two of you will be picked up by your webinar participants. A great co-host makes a webinar so much more fun and the enthusiasm will rub off on your webinar participants.

PRESENTATION PRACTICE and DELIVERY

> ***"It usually takes me more than three weeks to prepare a good impromptu speech."***
>
> *-Mark Twain*

Practice cannot be stressed enough. Think of yourself as the leading role in a Broadway production. You are not looking for audience applause: what you want is your desired outcome, which is for the participants to be active and buy (or to take the next step). Your replay gives you the encore. Engage the emotions of your participants.

If the idea of being the leading role in a Broadway production stresses you out, consider Olympic athletes. Olympic athletes have a routine they follow when getting ready for competition. In *The Webinar Way* interview with Ty Cohen, he describes his "pre-webinar" routine to get into the right state of mind. Your webinar IS a performance on a live event. Get over your performance anxiety with a planned routine before the event opens "live."

Plan ahead. Test and practice. You are "on stage" so get familiar with the webinar tools in advance.

Practice out loud. Record yourself and listen back. Listen to your tempo, your "ums" and "ahs," your breaths, and your pauses. Be aware of clearing your throat. Be conscious of your voice and PLEASE do not cough into the microphone. Move away or turn your head. Have a glass of water, or a few glasses of water, beside you. While you practice, say it aloud, as if you were telling the audience, "I'm going to take a quick drink of water." What you do in your practice helps you stay real and human.

The main reason you want to practice your presentation is to know your material thoroughly. Deliver the hook point during the open and close of your webinar during your practice runs.

The opening must be memorized and rehearsed. Closing must be fast paced and on target. The middle can be flawsome (flawed + awesome). People tend to judge you by your words, especially your first and last words. Don't be monotone and don't sound like you are reading. Own your words and delivery to create maximum impact.

Use a proactive pause to get attention and slow down a bit. Add this to your notes. Your pacing should be planned out. Don't bore your audience by reading bullet points because it is considered a "crime" if you are just "reading from the slides" without adding additional value.

Practice your pacing so you don't rush the essentials toward the end. Then you can turn your attention to The B-spot. The B-spot is the combination of the brain, mind and emotions.

Practice lets you focus on the details of your presentation. You need to **start the engines** of your participants' brains with compelling visuals. Add in content that engages the mind. Provide statistics or other shocking data that jolts the mind to attention. Create the open loop that opens a **big gap** that makes the participant say to themselves, "I need help," or, "I need this." Use evocative visuals to stimulate the emotion. Channel their desire. Channel and direct their focus on **one single action**, the action takes them to what you have defined as your outcome.

I remember watching a "behind the scenes" show on the making of a classic movie with actor Peter O'Toole. There was a set of clips, with no dialogue, with O'Toole simply using different facial expressions. This was all about eliciting emotion from the viewers. You want them HOT and excited! Turn on their B-Spot!

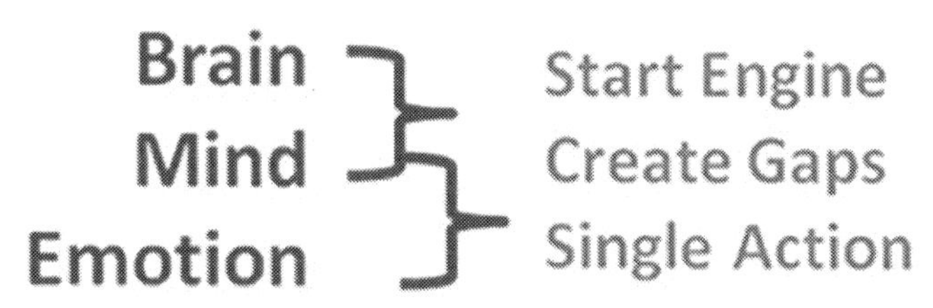

Figure 9

To quote Guy Kawasaki in reference to PowerPoint pitches:

"To cut to the chase, there are two extremes in online dating: eHarmony and Hot Or Not. When you use the former, you provide the data along twenty-nine dimensions to find your soul mate. When you use the latter, you look at a picture and decide if the person is "hot or not" in a few seconds.

When it comes to presentation, think Hot Or Not, not eHarmony."

The idea that Guy shares in the quote above are about the images you choose to support your dialogue, and those images should be HOT and evoke emotion. He is specifically referring to pitching for venture capital, for only 20 minutes, with only a handful of slides. Venture capital pitches are not the focus of *The Webinar Way*.

Your delivery depends on your practice. Your passion and enthusiasm will come through in your voice. When delivering, the quality of a presenter's voice is critical to portraying an air of authority and getting the message across. Your voice must deliver the message and not stand in the way of it. There is more about voice in Pillar 5, Power Position.

Your delivery is not just the close. How your presentation is structured, the valuable content and the flow of your presentation will make a big impact on the webinar participants.

You've got to get into the B-spot of your participants. Know their pain points, their frustration, deepest fears and desires. The lifestyle pictures and the "before and after" images will evoke emotion. Go on the roller coaster ride with them. Build rapport. Take them to the place where they can envision their gain point.

Yes, we all would like to think we are high-functioning evolved humans using our neo-cortex to process logical thought. The truth is our brain responds to motion 250 milliseconds before we logically know it is happening. Use this to your advantage in your presentation. Practice the transitions on your slides to call to mind the feelings that your perfectly "profiled" participant can relate to. The more emotion you channel, the greater the possibility of the action you want when you get to your pitch and close the webinar. Bring up the emotional threshold to channel the desire. Practice your emotion so it comes through in your voice.

This isn't the first place you are reading about practice. We also discussed practice in the planning section. Practice, obviously, is part of the rehearsal and dry runs of your presentation. Get help from a webinar coach.

A little twist on a familiar saying: "When you fail to practice, you plan to fail."

I like to say, **"Practice makes profit."**

The truth is: the more familiar you are with your material and with the other presenter's style, the better delivery and the better results you can expect from your webinar. It is worth repeating Joel Weldon's words, "Preparation compensates for lack of talent."

Prepare Your Environment

Practice on the same computer that you will be using when you go live.

Reboot your computer. Power down all other applications, especially instant messaging, email and anything that sends alerts and turn off pop-ups. Turn your mobile phone on vibrate just in-case your co-presenter must send a last minute text or during the presentation. Use two monitors if possible. Use a good quality microphone. If you are using Skype, change your status to "do not disturb."

If possible, set up a second computer (borrow one if you need to) to test your webinar presentation. Your webinar may look different on different sized screens, on faster or slower computers, with faster or slower Internet access, and/or other variables. Sharing your desktop is one of those variables because it takes a lot of bandwidth to copy your computer screen to the audience's screen—it can create a lag time.

What you see on your computer may not be what the audience sees on their screens. Having a second computer available is a great way to test this. Test on a PC and a Mac. It is also a great way to test microphones and speakers too.

Choose options for sharing: whole desktop, a section of the screen, application, or browser tabs, etc. Test everything, practice and practice again. Look over your practice recordings. You may find a few "webinar blooper" gems that you can laugh about and learn from, and possibly share on YouTube for some laughs.

PARTICIPANTS

> ***"A satisfied customer is the best business strategy of all."***

Participants' Perspective

Listen to the interview with Athena Davis, who was a webinar participant. She described her experience with urgency, scarcity and social proof. Athena's excitement, days after the webinar, came ringing through on the interview. She was not a "plant" in the audience, but she did "raise her hand" when asked if she wanted to speak.

You can invite current customers to participate to get the ball rolling with discussions and Q&As. They can also provide live testimonials. This ties in with the social proof that what you are offering really works.

You Want AP (not PA)

Interactivity turns passive attendees into active participants.

PA = passive attendees snooze

AP = active participants YES!

Active participants give you virtual applause. This is the "Stay Up" step you see in figure 1 in the Webinar Quick Start. Create the experience that gives rise to participation and applause for your webinar event. Converse and create engagement and you will quickly have active participants. Use your *F.A.M.E. examples* for dramatic effect. A webinar master who makes a pitch on every webinar sets up the ideal situation so that the AP "Active participants" all become AP "All Paying" customers who pay up.

To get your participants on the same virtual page as you, have them imagine what they can do with your product and how they see themselves using it. Put them into the situation of their current pain point and where they want to be when they gain the desired outcome.

Pain Point	**GAP**	**Gain Point**
Where They Are Now	*Close the Gap: What it Will Take to Get There?*	*Where They Want To Be*

The idea of a Pain Point refers to the tipping point of discomfort that precedes taking action to get to the Gain Point of where you want to be. Mentally take your webinar participants from their pain point to their gain point. You close the gap with the solution you are offering.

Participants may be a little overwhelmed with all the great content you are providing and might request a copy of your slide deck. The slides themselves (if done right) don't make good handouts. You need the corresponding commentary with the slides. Prepare a valuable handout or bonus instead that they can implement to get closer to their gain point.

Your co-presenter or moderator can answer participant questions via chat, serve up questions and comments to presenter via dialog, and even ask "planted questions." Everyone benefits from addressing common objections. Someone is surely thinking of it and, when you address the question, they don't feel like they are alone and they know they are on the right webinar. Definitely consider a Q&A session after the webinar closes because, very often, this is the time your webinar participants become very active and begin to engage and interact.

Participant and Presenter Interaction: Question and Answer Session

The optional Q&A session can last as little as 5 minutes to hours. Even if you have done a great job providing actionable valuable content and explained your offer so it is crystal clear, there will still be questions from webinar participants.

Some presenters never do a Q&A and others always do. It is highly recommended to do a Q&A session after your close. It will most likely lead to more sales. Ty Cohen said his longest Q&A session was a whole 70 minutes AFTER the webinar had ended. This resulted in nearly $100k in sales from that one webinar, within the first 22 hours (and that was BEFORE he sent out the replay). Then, with the replay, he brought in $200k the first week. Q&A can be the most important part of your webinar.

Do not make the mistake of only having someone answer questions in the chat box on the webinar platform. Repeat a question for everyone to hear so they have the aural connection and then answer it live. Answer as many questions as possible, even if you have to stay for an hour or more AFTER your presentation. You never know which question and corresponding answer may be the one that is the tipping point of the sale. Many presenters say that the longer they make the Q&A session, the more sales that are made for their product.

Question: Why do webinars work so well with today's busy prospects?

John Murphy, Lauren Goldstein, Loren McDonald, Remy Bergsma, John Anderson, Dennis Shiao, and Matt Goodwin all contributed on Focus.com to answer the following question (condensed and edited):

"Why do webinars work so well with today's busy prospects?"

This is a great question. Unfortunately, there is not a simple answer. I've engineered over 1,500 webinars and virtual events in the past three years. People come for more reasons than you would expect. Whether it is eLearning, prospecting, data sharing, knowledge exchange, or other various reasons, it all boils down to convenience.

In a world where everyone is an expert, who has time to read extensive blogs, catch-up on every status update, tweet, or reply, or, even worse, check the reliability of all of these sources? Social media numbness...

Webinars offer three benefits to the participants: On Demand content any time during the replay period; a live exchange with the subject matter expert on live days launches; and mobility if the webinar platform is capable.

Another reason is that a lot of people may only get to attend one industry conference per year, so webinars are another way of getting exposed to content that they would see at industry events but don't, because of travel costs and schedule conflicts.

Why webinars are 1-hour long is an interesting question. Video best practices for audience retention call for 18-30 minutes of highly engaging content. Most webinars are one hour long because it allows the producer a larger window of time to capture additional audience members. As a participant, if I get an urgent request during the webinar, I have more time to respond before the live Q&A opportunity in my webinar.

I've personally presented/co-presented or moderated 60+ Webinars and one of the things I've learned is that each webinar participant brings a personal agenda to their attendance. They usually were attracted to the webinar topic for a specific reason and see it as a way of getting free online training or "free consulting" and to have nagging questions answered by an expert.

I think most companies have recognized that the best way to approach webinar content is from a "trends and tips" perspective – keeping the commercials secondary and to a minimum. So webinar participants now expect that most of them will be primarily educational and not hour-long product sales pitches.

I believe webinars fail to attract attendees because the title, content or speaker is not compelling enough. Do not create a webinar if it is just a sales commercial. Segment the content and let the audience drive the conversation by using interactive chats and other forms of interactive engagement. This will pull the audience in and lessen the chance of it being viewed as an hour-long sales pitch.

Attendance numbers indicate 40% – 60% of registrants never show up live. This is because life gets in the way. Most business webinars are conducted during the day. What happens during the day? E-mails, meetings, client issues, team support, and various other activities that may intrude on your webinar time.

Webinars are a great tactic at any stage in the buying cycle (as long as the topic is well defined and the description is accurate, such that the target prospects know what they'll be getting).

I think the reason that webinars work is that the buyers are looking and listening and not feeling any pressure to purchase, and, as a consequence, are more open to what is being suggested in the webinar. Also, with many of the webinars, you can view them at a time that suits you; many are pre-recorded and then can be viewed on demand. A good webinar is very compelling, as you have the undivided attention of the participant.

I think one of the most underestimated reasons for the popularity of webinars is simply the dedicated time slot, because it is an event. It is easy to blow off reading a lengthy blog post or white paper, but when you have a webinar on your calendar for 1:00 pm on Tuesday, you will be more likely to commit to it.

This page intentionally left blank

PILLAR 5: POWER POSITION

> ***"The greatness of a man is... in his ability to affect those around him positively."***
>
> *- Bob Marley*

Presence, Prize, Persuasion, Power Position

- **Presence:** How do you create a commanding presence to be seen as an authority?
- **Prize:** What are the different types of "prizing" as part of the webinar experience?
- **Persuasion:** What forms of persuasion turn participants into buyers and raving fans?
- **Power Position:** What is the Ultimate Power Position?

PRESENCE: Sex Appeal of the Webinar Presenter

Your Power Position is your presence and that can be summed up simply as "sex appeal." In the physical world, sex appeal is defined as a quality of being attractive that seems to ooze out.

Sex appeal on a webinar is an attractiveness or charisma that can inspire devotion in others. On a webinar, the sex appeal factor exists because of the authority you command, the celebrity you create and fame that ensues. Many people become famous on webinars and that creates even more sex appeal.

Previously, my other life as the *Love Linguist* gives me the authority and knowledge about the in-depth details of intimate sex appeal. That is a one-to-one experience.

We all know that webinars are a one-to-many experience. A great webinar presenter makes the participants feel it is a one-to-one experience. You create a compelling connection. You leave a great impression because of your professional webinar delivery.

To stay in the Power Position, you need to know about psychology and physiology.

YOUR PSYCHOLOGY

Fear or Confidence Scale: There are two extremes for new webinar presenters. It is a big mistake to be one or the other.

You can be in complete fear about speaking, about presenting in a new environment, or about using webinar technology. This state will not serve you or others.

Or, you can have no fear at all. If this is you, you may not be willing to improve, work with a mentor, learn something different or get additional training.

The good news is, if you are reading this book, you are most likely somewhere in between fearful and confident and you are willing to learn, explore and improve.

Listen to *The Webinar Way* interview with Tony Laidig who describes in detail how he got over his fear and went on to do over 500 webinars. He was scared initially, but went forward anyway and now clearly is in the Power Position on his webinars.

Become the Prize: Being the Prize is an attitude. You invest time, resources and energy into the presentation, the promotion, and the follow-up. When you do this for your intended audience, your attitude comes through in the way you provide value. Give incredible value and exceed your participant's expectations.

Part of the reason you become the "prize" is because of the status you command as the webinar presenter. Participants want access to you. That puts you in the Power Position. People want to buy what you have to offer. People want to work with you and associate with you. Become a pro at being "the Prize."

The webinar presenter is the star performer. Yes, you can deliver a stellar presentation! Think Rockstar!

When Technology Threatens to Take Over

Technology. Sometimes you are the master, sometimes you are the slave. A webinar platform depends on three parts of technology: the webinar platform itself, your computer, and your Internet connection.

Latency and choppiness do happen on webinars. Sometimes the voice commentary does not sync-up with the slide. We mentioned that you should keep your cell phone on vibrate for text messages from co-presenters or your assistant. Online webinar events are subject to things going wrong just like physical events. Set up an emergency plan and communicate it to all hosts, presenters and moderators. Know what you will do if you lose internet connection, there is a computer crash, presenter loses audio, a screen goes blank, etc.

Keep your cool. Stay in the Power Position when the technology goes awry and don't let the technology get the better of you. Your Q&A will begin to fill up describing the technical issue when trouble starts, so keep an eye on the text coming in. Ask for a simple sound test "type yes if you can hear me" and watch if most people type yes. The one person who can't hear you probably needs to adjust their volume or computer sound settings. Have you moderator help with these issues.

Stay calm. Don't let setbacks stop you from reaching your desired outcome. Stay in the Power Position and don't point fingers or blame.

PERSUASION

Psychology and Your Participants. You need to know your target audience. Know how you benefit them and know their minds.

When you feel confident in the value you provide, you indoctrinate and teach attendees to accept your training. Wyatt Woodsmall said, *"When you can articulate a person's problem better than they can, they automatically and unconsciously credit you with knowing the solution."* A webinar is an indoctrination mechanism that showcases who you are and proves you are the one who helps your audience. It gets you in the power position.

When you present and your webinar audience hears you, it is their interests, ideas, fears, desires, wishes, aspirations, doubts, hopes, and ambitions to which you are speaking. You skyrocket your position of power and you are accepted as an authority. You present with confidence because you have specific knowledge about your participants. Be proud of the webinar content you have created and inspire confidence with your knowledge. That knowledge is in sync with what the participants think, how they feel, and what they truly, deeply want.

Know Your Participants. Review your prospective customer profile and refine it. The more refined and specific this is, the easier it will be to speak to their needs. Make absolutely sure you know their needs, wants and desires. What does a "win" look like for them?

Know How You Can Benefit Your Participants – What are Your Benefits? You must have an outcome for your webinar. You acknowledge and give recognition to participants for showing up and you identify with them. That lets them know that they are on the right webinar and you understand their issues and problems. They must have a need — a burning desire — for what you are offering. You help uncover it and go deeper.

To help them, take those needs, wants, and desires and show your potential customer how your product or service can fill their need and solve their problem.

Dave Sheahan, who has created a program called *6 Weeks to a Cover Model Body*, is a firm believer in webinars because he can show the before and after photos of his clients as social proof, and it works well along with the dialogue. It makes it real. Listen to Dave's interview on *The Webinar Way.*

A BENEFIT is: "look great in that bikini" or "get a cover model body in 6 weeks."

A benefit is NOT: "help you eat less calories" or "help you lose weight."

Know Their Minds. Understand the mind of your prospective customer. – It is critical to understand how a member of your target audience thinks about the need/problem and, particularly, the solution that will help them achieve THEIR goal.

What are their hot buttons? What are their issues? What will trigger them?

Understanding the way they think about it will help you properly keep their attention and lead them to the close. That's the easiest way to persuade.

When you know their motivations, your persuasion is seamless because you are addressing their underlying needs. What are her fears and frustrations? What is he motivated by? Is there a problem they are trying to solve? Is there an underlying passion your service or product can help fulfill?

This may be a review of salesmanship and marketing 101, but let's assume your product or service is a vehicle to help your ideal customer accomplish something they want. Here are some examples:

- You are a photographer who helps people create cherished moments that last forever.
- You are a coach or consultant who helps people achieve their goals financially, personally, or with their business.

- You own a gym that helps people look better, feel better, and become healthier.
- You are a professional advisor who helps get people out of sticky situations, through tough times, or maybe helps them with large financial transactions and decisions.

What are they REALLY LOOKING FOR?

- Your potential "customer" is not looking for a gym, a photographer, a consultant, pest control, a carpet cleaner, an attorney, or a CPA. **They are looking to solve their problem, relieve their pain, accomplish a goal, or fulfill a passion.**
- People are not looking to buy a drill—they are looking to drill a hole. They want the result.
- People are looking for systems and steps that clearly will get them to their desired goal.

When you build a persuasive presentation, establish that there is a problem upfront because this helps convince your webinar participants that they need to make a change. Use the context of comparison such as "before and after" or "advantage and disadvantage" to help people see the change they want to achieve. Identify situations and various actions in a cause and effect scenario to show different actions to solve a problem. Lead them to your solution.

In Pillar 1: Perspective, we talked about what people want. When it comes to the Internet, people want to know how to do something the easiest, quickest, and cheapest way with the greatest return on time and investment.

Your ability to persuade has everything to do with understanding the needs and emotions of your participants.

When they feel you know their situation, and have empathy for them, you can ethically persuade them.

Cater to their motivations. If you have a great offer that caters to the inner motivations of your potential customer and you give a free gift when they register for the webinar, then you are starting the game with a chance to win. Then it will be up to you to continue building that relationship with your new prospect who has signed-up for the webinar. Throughout the webinar, begin building trust, building up your authority, and building rapport. At the close of your webinar, give them an irresistible offer. Use your webinars to help your participants solve a problem they're having. Establish trust and credibility, which are two attributes that are key if you want somebody to purchase from you eventually. When people trust you, they are attracted to your offers, consume your content, and buy your products. The best way to build trust is through high-quality content marketing particularly webinars. They recommend you to others.

Give your webinar participants inspiration that will raise their ambition. Paint pictures with your visuals and your words about a future that (with your product benefits) will get them closer to their own goals and dreams. Extend those benefits into other areas in their life: in a social context, family life, professional life, their free time and personal choices.

If you and your service are the Prize, it is easy to stay in the Power Position. If you are selling a product, the product is an extension of your expertise, which also keeps you in the Power Position. People will want a piece of you! The proximity to you is valuable to clients.

If you are a personality-driven brand and you deliver on your promises, your customers will spread the word. There will be a few active customers who are your raving fans. Use *F.A.M.E. examples* from your story and storyboarding process in Pillar 4. Word of mouth will take off and sound bites will spread. Take care of these buyers and foster your relationship with them.

More on the idea of "being the Prize" in the next pages.

Different Types of "Prizing" As Part of The Webinar Experience

Let's look again at a few webinar formats and the different types of *prizing*:

Awareness and Positioning Webinars. If you are entering a new market or want to expand as a personality-based brand, such as a coach, mentor, advisor, consultant, expert or guru, this type of marketing webinar can generate new leads or help qualify current leads by identifying a level of interest. Your webinar is an excellent way to promote useful content and teach timely topics and get exposure. Set the stage to introduce later an opportunity to work directly with the presenter and have a lot of interaction with the presenter. ***You are the Prize!***

Educational Webinars. Provides prospects with new information or helps them better understand a specific set of problems and solutions. As Sean Vosler says, "People don't buy when they understand you and your product, they buy when they understand their own needs and themselves. You spotlight what their needs are and how your product helps them." ***You have the prize solution!*** **The person who can articulate the problem the clearest is seen to be the person who also has the answer.**

Demonstration Webinars. Demos of software solutions and software tools (such as social media interfaces and dashboards) are perfect for webinar show and tell. Even if you are the presenter on behalf of another company you still ***become a celebrity.*** (However, it may be the status of "micro-celebrity" in your marketplace.)

Paid Webinar. Your participants pay to attend as part of a webinar series or membership. ***You are the authority.***

It is the content subject matter that will attract attention in your webinar promotions. Be clear in your webinar registration about what participants can expect and deliver on it. If you are a personality-based brand, it also gives you a chance to establish your authority to those who might not know who you are yet. If you've already established your sex appeal, then your existing fans will attend your webinar because they already know, trust and like you.

PRESENCE and YOUR POWER POSITION

> ***"One measure of your PRIZE FACTOR is the caliber of people who choose to follow you."***
>
> *- Sherrie Rose*

In the physical world, the body language a person projects around them is their presence. How you stand, hold your head, walk and make eye contact with others creates attraction.

Offline and online, a commanding presence is when a person projects confidence and charisma which causes others to see them in an approving way. People want to know you and work with you.

When your webinar event grabs the attention of your participants, then the excitement and good feelings generated can be transferred to you, the presenter, in the Power Position. If you are presenting a series of webinars, your overarching theme will help you create mind-share and further define those feelings in the webinar prospect and participants' minds. There is continuity with the content and the presenter. There is an instant recognition of status when you are in the Power Position. As the person in the Power Position, you have to protect your position.

- You have to be approachable but not readily available.
- You have established your credibility and are seen as an expert authority.
- You have something great to offer and selling will not make a difference to you, but the offer, if purchased, will make a difference to them.
- You have to be able to walk away so-to-speak from the sale.
- You control the experience and emphasize specific viewpoints.
- You activate the reactive B-spot triggers (they are compelled to react).
- You are prepared to answer objections using fun and humor (you respond).
- You know how to tease your audience.
- You have sex appeal with an air of boldness.
- You are chased by prospective customers.

To be in the Power Position, the webinar presenter must know the triggers that cause action. You control the frame (which, with slides, makes it so much easier) and you control the experience. The triggers to action have a physiological component.

PHYSIOLOGY

Standing can boost your energy. Print your slides with the presenter notes. Practice, know your slides, use a printout, and focus on the interactivity tools to engage your participants. Know all your anecdotes, extra annotations, and use the special reminders that are right in front of you. If the visuals freeze, you can still carry on verbally so there is an aural connection.

Before a webinar, if you drink coffee or soda, lay off the caffeine and sugar as this affects your B-spot and adrenaline. Don't eat salty food beforehand as that will dry out your mouth. BREATHE. Before you start, get in the right physical state. Slow down, enunciate your words and don't speak too quickly, except during the close when a faster pace can incite people to act on your offer.

Sound. Your voice is important. Your voice should change, modulate, louder and software depending on what you are emphasizing. Keep participants engaged by just changing the speed of your delivery. Slow down and speed up. Slowing down to explain more difficult concepts and speed up to explain why the concepts are important and how to apply them. There are successful webinar presenters with annoying voices whose products are so stellar that people still buy. If you can, get a voice coach to improve your voice if you have been told your voice is annoying.

There are six handy vocal warm-up exercises recommended by Julian Treasure. Go look up Ted talk *Julian*

Treasure How to speak so that people want to listen. The vocal exercises start at minute 7:50 if you want to skip ahead.

Motion

Motion catches the eye. Movement keeps the B-spot active and the eyes of your webinar participants on the screen. That is why all the movement built-in to software like Prezi and SlideRocket makes them popular for delivering presentations because it makes it more like *show-ware.*

Change is the best remedy for boredom. Make one point or less per slide. Use more slides for a visually appealing slideshow, but not to just fill time unnecessarily on your webinar.

Do you want your participants just listening and multi-tasking while traveling down Distraction Avenue, or do you want to guide them along The Webinar Way? If there is a lot of visual change and motion, we notice it because our B-spot is wired for change. We don't want to miss something good. Appeal to the persuasion tactic that, if the participant looks away, they'll miss out. Be strategic.

Back to the B-spot. I agree with the experts from all over the world who say the most sensitive and responsive zone of a person's body is the brain, what I fondly call the B-spot. The B-spot (brain/mind/emotion) is always a factor in a selling situation – to buy or not to buy. People need to be aroused to buy and take action. The brain makes decisions seven seconds before an action is taken. We tend to dislike something before we like it. The more someone has to think about a decision, using the higher brain functions in the neo-cortex, the more excuses you create for a webinar participant to not act on your offer. The more abstract the concept, the more confusion and the more excuses you create will keep participants in non-action mode.

Use analogy and metaphor to make abstract concepts simple and test to remove all confusion. Clear concepts put you in the Power Position because you know how to make the complex simple, and people will want to follow your expertise. Analogy and metaphor should be designed to evoke emotion. Get their attention, activate memories because they influence action, and use emotion to bring participants to a decision point.

Creating surprise, in the form of shock and awe or a big "Aha! moment," jolts the webinar participant out of the passive "I already know that" state into one of alertness. Before and after images are powerful. Use a F.A.M.E. example.

You can use trends or statistics: **Global e-commerce sales will be nearly 4.48 trillion US dollars in 2021, almost 20% per year growth.** A Gallup poll revealed that **"fully engaged" clients spend an average of 56% more money than those without emotional connections.**

Emotion. The B-spot plays a huge role in love. I studied the love bio-chemicals to understand how they work in love relationships, especially the pleasure bio-chemical, dopamine. The love bio-chemicals are neurotransmitters in the brain. Surprise and novelty stimulate dopamine production.

The bio-chemical of alertness is norepinephrine and it creates tension with fear of loss, harmful consequences or conflict. It is a pain point. On a purely survival basis, this is like the wild tiger coming closer to you that triggers the fear of being eaten alive. When you add scarcity tactics, like limited-time offers at the close of your webinar, the norepinephrine kicks-in, creating tension in the process.

In the business setting, the bio-chemicals dopamine and norepinephrine can help you get the attention of your webinar participants. Here's how they work:

- Channeling desire activates the bio-chemical dopamine, triggered by reward – that's a gain (like pleasure).
- Creating tension activates the bio-chemical norepinephrine, triggered by scarcity – that's a loss (like pain).

We discussed pain points and gain points earlier. Use images and words that put webinar participants into the situation of their current pain point that creates tension, and channel their desire with the opportunity that comes from your solution that takes them where they want to be in their life or business situation.

Channel Desire + Create Tension = Capture Attention

You need to channel desire and create tension and create push-pull to keep attention. Oren Klaff calls channeling desire "hot cognition." The B-spot is hot with desire. The visuals in your presentation and your voice will get you closer to your outcome. When Oren was pitching for an airport facility, he used lots of aviation porn (*his words*) in his presentation.

What images will bring up emotion triggers in your webinar participants? Combine and contrast images of what their future could look like, as well as dismal situations if they don't make any change to their current status. Contrast past and future.

During the close, take the webinar participants on an emotional ride with conflicting tension that shows up subtly in their body, with the chance of reward. Hold off just short of safety and show them that the way they get to that safe place of reward is within reach with the purchase of your offer. The count-down timer is like a tiger coming closer and closer and, to relieve that tension, your webinar participant must take action and get to safety.

You want your participant to react, not think, and take immediate action. Your irresistible offer should be acted-on with an impulse to buy that quickly will take them to their gain point. Move your participants from what "is" to what "could be" and what they will gain. Move them to the future they desire.

Be the Prize – The Ultimate Power Position

Connect with Your Participants. A webinar presenter blends charisma and thought leadership. You are, after all, leading the webinar. It is a combination of your personality (voice, humor, and influence) and your knowledge and thoughts (content).

When prospects and customers see YOU AS THE PRIZE, you are clearly in the Power Position. This translates into sales when you get to the close portion of your webinar.

If you connect well with your customers, you're already "the Prize" and people follow you, almost regardless of your content. You have established yourself. If they have become a true fan, you are the Prize, because they want to be in your social circle. They may not need proof to register for your webinar and buy your product. Ardent fans will identify with the content promoted on a webinar and be quickly swayed, mainly by your charisma and magnetic personality.

Present powerful benefits. While it helps to be an influential person and to be a great speaker, you can still become the PRIZE when you offer powerful benefits and you are perceived as the expert authority—a thought leader with the know-how and answers. You'll be seen as the person in the Power Position. Listen to *The Webinar Way* interview with Scott Rewick who sells a $10K package on his webinar that includes a private mastermind and special events.

Connect with Content. If people don't know who you are, then your message must provide hard evidence (solid content) to influence people. Don't assume everyone knows you, even if you have a big following.

We are living in a knowledge-driven world, and prospective followers and customers respect their own knowledge and won't listen to claims not based on solid evidence. Your content must be excellent!

Prize and Personal Appeal. First, as humans, emotional engagement and personal attraction will never disappear. Second, in fields where values carry more weight than facts, a charismatic presenter can win large followings. In the soft subjects, such as the personal development arena, it is hard to prove that one method will work better than another and many personal development coaches have very similar methods. So, that's what it comes down to: personal appeal and impact.

Prizing is based on power. Being in the Power Position, and being perceived as "the Prize," means you have stellar content, you connect with your audience and you are a powerful closer. Your participants want premium access to you.

This page intentionally left blank

PILLAR 6: PITCH

> ***"If you help people make a decision to do something that makes their life better, you're a good closer."***
>
> *- Kevin Nations*

Profit Models, Promise, Pacing, Pitch Examples

- **Profit Models:** What are the different types of profit models for webinars?
- **Promise:** Why does a webinar pitch start with a promise?
- **Pacing:** How do you set the pace of your voice and energy, especially during the close?
- **Pitch Examples:** How do you use trial closes, decoys, stacking, proof, scarcity, clarity and closing statements to turn your webinar into a profit machine?

We talked about being in the Power Position that activates the B-spot (mind/brain/emotions) to create a reaction that is emotionally-based. You take people from their pain point to their gain point and help people discover their needs.

Profit Models

With money-making webinars, first of all, someone has to sell something. Second of all, there must be a defined target audience for the webinar, whether it's your customer base or someone else's, such as with a joint venture.

Four Categories of Webinar Profit Models

1. Your Product/Service *(Your intellectual property)*
2. Other People's Product/Service *(As Affiliate or Representative)*
3. Joint Venture Webinars & Online Summits *(We discuss this in Pillar 7)*
4. Automated Webinars *(We discuss this in The Webinar Lifestyle)*

Webinar Profit Models

A. Your Own Product

You are the presenter and own the product or service that is being sold. You sell directly to your own customer base. You can sell sponsorships. You can charge for the webinar. You can offer the product or service directly. Live and encore recordings.

B. Other People's Product/Service

You present and represent other people's products on a webinar. You can do this as a webinar presenter, webinar manager, or webinar producer. Live and replay. You can also license other people's webinars, include them in your marketing funnel and translate them into different languages.

C. Joint Venture Webinar & Summits

You are a Webinar Joint Venture Broker or you have JV brokers finding matching customer lists for related products for your customers. Webinar JV brokers find, secure, license, and establish JV Partnerships. Joint ventures are also used in single-day or multi-day Webinar Summits. Live and replay.

D. Automated Webinar Systems

You have a high converting webinar and set it up on "auto-pilot." You can also license other people's webinars and include them in your marketing funnel. Recorded.

Additional Profits: Repurposing Webinar Content

You can also profit and benefit from repurposing content. What does "repurpose the webinar content" mean? It simply means reusing the content for different purposes. For example:

- **Recording.** Sell the webinar recording or give away as a bonus. You can sell the webinar as a DVD or provide it as a member benefit.
- **Video.** Your webinar could be turned into video clips for your website, blog or YouTube. Choose and segment the snippets wisely. Use your F.A.M.E. examples.

- **Audio.** Sell the webinar MP3 or give it away as a bonus. You can sell the webinar audio as a CD or, even better, on a USB drive.
- **Transcript.** Sell the webinar transcript or give it away as a bonus.
- **Text.** The webinar audio transcript can be used to create articles for your blog. Turn its content into an email. Create an eBook, checklists, or mind maps based on the webinar content. Include links to your upcoming webinar registration page or email opt-in page.
- **Notes.** Summary and key points of the webinar. Can be used as lead candy gifts and magnets on landing pages.
- **Bonuses.** Provide repurposed content as an accompanying bonus for a membership site, a digital product, or another webinar. Get creative.

All of these repurposed formats can be used as upsells and standalone products.

Breaking Down The Types of Webinars

There may be four categories of webinar profit models but there are several different types of money-related webinars. Each type can fall into almost any of the four categories, and not all produce a direct financial profit. Some are purely for lead generation, brand building and customer loyalty.

1. **Demo "Show and Tell" Webinars** (technical, software, systems)
2. **Paid Webinar** (singles, series and bundles)
3. **Strategy Session: Free training followed by a consultation or discovery call** (coaching, consulting)

4. **Free Intro Webinar with Paid Webinar Series**
5. **Information Products and Upsell Webinars**
6. **Customer Loyalty** (retention, training)
7. **Awareness and Positioning Webinars** (authority and brand-building)
8. **Educational Webinars** (lead generation)
9. **Local Business Webinars** (lead generation, service offer)
10. **Affiliate Marketing Webinar** (other people's product or service)
11. **Network Marketing Webinar** (other people's product or service)
12. **Auction Webinars** (your own and other people's product or services)
13. **Interview Style Webinar** (other people's product or service)

Webinars level up your list building. Even if you're not sure you have the right content to deliver, you can get started by interviewing other experts on webinars because this in itself will increase your perceived authority, your power position, and build your audience. Many online summits use the interview format.

5 MAIN TYPES OF MONEY-MAKING WEBINARS

Webinars can be implemented in your business model to generate leads, create instant authority and credibility, drive sales, attract raving fans and sell to repeat customers.

We've mentioned 13 types of webinars above, and several of them, such as Local Business Webinars, **Awareness and Positioning Webinars, Educational Webinars, and Strategy Session webinars are designed for lead generation primarily as a two-step process that will eventually lead to making money**. Also, depending on how you define it, some types can really fall under the same type such as affiliate marketing and network marketing. There is overlap, but it is your monetization path and your purpose that defines your webinar.

1. DEMO – SHOW AND TELL WEBINAR

The show and tell webinar is quite simple. All we do is take a product or service that we have and show it off on the Internet, using some presentation slides combined with a live online DEMO via the webinar platform. The demo is great if you have a software product or you want to show a peek inside a member's area. You are in essence sharing your screen with the participants. The participants will see your screen as if they are sitting beside you while you are demonstrating the key features. It's a very, very powerful way to sell with the show and tell webinars.

Many people show how to use free services that may appear to be complicated. How to Get the Best from Twitter, Facebook, and WordPress are popular categories. These are designed to get coaching clients or students who want the training in a password protected members area.

The show and tell webinar is compelling and creates instant authority. Remember to show only 3-5 key areas, otherwise it becomes overwhelming. There is overlap in the type of webinar styles and often a Show and Tell webinar is perfect for a joint venture. Coaches and experts use the show and tell webinar.

2. PAY TO ATTEND WEBINAR

Matt Gillogly, who works with Perry Matthews, the Google Adwords expert, believes in the paid webinar. It is a nominal fee of about $25. The information on the webinar could be considered free education because there is an upsell at the end, but he says the $25 brings quality and qualified participants.

Listen to Matt's interview recorded as part of this book's resources.

If you are providing timely information, training on complex software or the market values what you are offering, you can charge for attendance. Prospects buy a ticket to attend and the price can be at whatever price your prospect expects for the value you are offering.

You can offer a series of single webinars or a bundle price if they want to attend all at a discount.

3. PAID WEBINAR SERIES

Listen to *The Webinar Way* interview with Tony Laidig on how he got started with his paid webinar series. He has conducted hundreds of webinars. Tony offers a free introductory webinar followed by a paid webinar series.

Wise people know that you can conduct great webinars, record them, and then create access to the recordings in a membership only website. Members pay to get an account to access all the content. Some folks deliver the webinar videos via Dropbox.

You can charge for the webinars at the time they are conducted to participate. It is easy for attendees to pay for the series if you use a registration page that has integration with your shopping cart or PayPal.

Building and launching a webinar series can be a lot like doing a product launch. It combines a product launch with a live event. As we discussed in Pillar 1, there are several parts to be played and one key role is the webinar project manager or producer. The webinar series creates the "product" from your live and recorded webinars.

For your product, you may wish to create a membership site, physical CDs and DVDs, or a USB drive/card. Whichever method you prefer, a webinar series is the way to go. If you are an author of a book that has subject matter that can be turned into training, you can offer a paid webinar series. It can be anywhere from a couple of webinars up to a 12-part series, or possibly more. You can segment the webinar training by chapters in the book or main sections. After editing, you can put it into a membership area or automate the delivery if the content is evergreen, meaning it will not go out-of-date. If it is technology-based, it will always be changing.

Some authors create a free webinar series. At the end of the series they offer coaching or some other service. Get creative!

If you add interviews on the subject, and add those to your membership area, the value goes up and your customers will be happy to pay a monthly fee to get the recordings. The information has to be current. Some people charge a nominal yearly fee for memberships and offer content that keeps them "on your list." People stay subscribed if you offer real value. Adding recorded webinars to your membership site every month is a huge benefit and a great way to keep clients subscribed to the membership site, because they know there's something new coming.

Many people with membership sites are selling a free trial upfront or a free membership level. Sell your product then give them a free member trial, because someone who has purchased the product is more likely to take the free trial and more likely to stay on after the free trial for a fixed period. Then offer the full membership. This type of continuity must be explained properly, which can be done starting with an email that takes them to an automated webinar or explainer video.

4. INFO PRODUCTS and UPSELLS WEBINAR

Your purpose of conducting a webinar is to turn your webinar into a product. This content keeps you in the mind's eye of your target market. Your webinar becomes a hub for your content factory. Here are a few ideas for repurposing content from your webinars.

- A well-converting single webinar can become a product you can use in an automated webinar.
- You can also separate the audio for a downloadable MP3, CD or podcast.
- You can segment the webinar in 2-5 minute sections and post on video sharing sites like YouTube. Using the right keywords, it will drive traffic back to your main website.
- You can have your webinars transcribed and use the text on article sharing sites, in eBooks or in reports to give away. Make sure that it is properly edited. You can outsource this work to freelancers.

You can also use webinars as an upsell tool. You can provide a free webinar as part of the upsell of another product, or you can offer a paid webinar. This upsell can be an exclusive offer to purchasers of another product. The customer benefits and you are seen as the authority. If it is a paid webinar upsell, you also benefit financially. Include access to the replay if you are doing the webinar live. And then on the automated webinar, you can offer another upsell if it makes sense. Upsells are great for selling high priced items.

5. CUSTOMER LOYALTY WEBINAR

Dax Aurand conducted show-and-tell demo webinars for his software product that sold for $997. He started doing customer training webinars to demo the product and answer questions. These demos reinforced the value of the software and dropped the refund rate to almost zero. Any webinar that keeps your earned money in your bank account is an excellent webinar.

Customer loyalty tactics are money keeping tactics. It may not be the webinar itself but rather what you do for the purchasing customers after your webinar; send them a thank you as a reciprocity tactic. Sean Malarkey sent his clients a box of fancy brownies after they purchased from the webinar. One particular customer wanted to send back the product but, because he ate the brownies, he felt obligated to keep the product and the eaten brownies were an incentive to go through the program.

YOUR PITCH STARTS WITH "A PROMISE"

> ***"Always be ready to sell, but never be selling."***
>
> *- Chris Brogan*

You make a promise at the beginning of the webinar and, as a person of integrity, you fulfill your promise and ask the webinar participants (before you begin the close portion of the webinar) if you kept your promise. It keeps you honest and your participants see you kept your word to them.

Your promise must deliver "Quick Action" content that allows people to take IMMEDIATE action after the webinar. People want to see RESULTS as quickly as possible, even if they don't buy the product. Give them something that they can implement. If they do buy, it is critical to have a well laid-out "Quick Start Action Plan" so the customer psychologically sees their purchase as making sense, and being able to realize how quickly their investment could be paid for, just by implementing the information. The more you focus on helping your customer get these results as quickly as possible, the more your customers will love you, and the less likely they will be to request a refund.

For your business to thrive, you need one thing: paying customers. Danny Iny says that salesmanship is what remains constant. So you must sell. If you're uncertain or uneasy when pitching your offer, then it's time to learn how to have sales conversations and close the sale.

Four advantages will help move the sale or action along when you can overcome the obstacle. I will use the example of the training program the Power of Webinars.

Ease? How much effort and work are you willing to put out to create a webinar that sells? *(It will take focused effort but you will be guided along)*

Speed? How long will it take to create the presentation? *(It can take as little as 29 days but realistically over 45 days.)*

Risk? Can you be assured that your investment will work for you? *(An expert webinar coach will guide you, you'll have all the tools you need and you are vital to your success.)*

Impact? Can you truly make a positive impact on others with the message in your webinar? *(Your passion and purpose with a good story and a well-matched, attentive audience help you win.)*

Keep these four advantages in mind and be true to your offer during the webinar close.

Your promise starts with your participant's eyes. Your first slide must ROCK! It must be eye-catching, provocative, and create curiosity. You must start with your hook. In Pillar I, in the People section, we spoke about profiling, which is creating the avatar of the person you have attracted to your webinar. Your hook must grab your prospect immediately and show value.

You want to get in the Power Position and state who this webinar is for and who it is not for. In the Introduction portion of your webinar, establish who you are talking to upfront and identify the benefits of what they will discover by participating on the webinar. Identify their problem.

As you go through the content portion of your webinar, continue to focus on as many benefits as possible that your webinar participants can enjoy. Remember: it is all about them.

Keep in mind that you want to be teaching and enrolling throughout the webinar. Your content delivery must also create desire and gaps so when you get to the transition the participants are primed to buy.

PACING

Inserting transition slides for questions and actions keeps participants engaged. They also know they can relax their B-spot while a question is posed and answered. It also gives a break with an opportunity to summarize with a quick recap, which drives home the core value proposition. Remember: it is your energy in delivering your content that the participants feed off. Include several of your well-selected mini-stories and F.A.M.E. examples that support your point and trigger emotional responses. The more emotional, the stronger and longer it will be retained by the webinar participant.

Insert a pregnant pause… to deliver massive impact. The B-spot is wired to pick up big and small changes, and that creates alertness. Those who are not paying attention will experience a "pattern interrupt" and will come back to focus on the presentation.

Be aware of your tempo.

Don't draw attention to a mistake or a problem that YOU notice in your webinar presentation, because most people are unaware of it. If you see a typo on the screen, or notice that a slide is out of order, go with the flow. Use a value judgment before apologizing for something barely anyone notices.

Pacing is about a sense of timing during the webinar. As a co-host, you may follow a set of tasks as part of the preparation of the webinar. Know the flow and order of execution of the tasks. Know the structure, content and flow of the webinar. Plan sections that would feel natural to be spontaneous and use it for engaging the participants.

If there seems to be a delay in the slides, and you have a co-host or moderator, say… "On the next slide you will see…" Hopefully, the moderator is paying attention and that will cue them to take action. They'll keep their own cool and perhaps pose questions in an impromptu Q&A to continue with the audio presentation if the visuals need technical assistance.

Tune into the emotional radar of your webinar participants so that you are central to their perception. You want them watching your screen intently and not being distracted. You can include a few testimonials or case studies throughout your presentation to support your close.

You want to amplify your voice and speed up your pacing in the close portion of your webinar. The beginning of your webinar and the ending of your webinar are the most important, so have these sections well scripted and rehearsed.

Many people drop off at the close portion of the webinar but, if you have incentivized them to stay with a bonus they receive at the end of the webinar, they will hear your pitch. Your energy, louder voice, fast pace, excitement and social proof will bring in more sales.

PITCH: Points of Action

There are various subtle points of action throughout your content portion, using trial closes to get buy-ins, "yes" agreements and to move them further along the process. The close is a way to connect and build rapport. Remember what Matt Gillogly said in his *The Webinar Way* interview: "A close is simply taking someone to the next stage in your process." You guide the webinar participants to the point of action, which is the next stage in the process. Typically, the final point of action is to click to go to a specific web link.

A trained webinar presenter makes an invisible transition from the content portion to the close portion of the webinar where you make your offer. At this point you have built upon your content and you have developed a significant connection with the webinar participants, and they are ready for more of what you have to offer.

Part of your original promise is to deliver actionable content your webinar participants can immediately implement when they get off the webinar and see a result in minutes, which gives them instant gratification. In a trial close, you ask if they can do it themselves and if they have everything they need to get started now. You want them to be saying "yes," mentally. You can also ask them to respond in the chat box with a specific comment.

The trial closes refer back to something you have promised. Jason Fladlien defines three trial closes that contain a form of a question, which can include a confirmation of what was just learned, the benefits, a time factor, and a call to action.

Trial close 1: ASK (after showing something powerful) — "So when are you going to do this?"

Trial close 2: STATEMENT + ASK — "You can see if you did [*insert technique*] ALONE, that could [*insert benefit*] couldn't it?" THEN you follow it up with "So when are you going to do this?"

Trial close 3: SHOW, STOP, CONTINUE — You share a powerful piece of information, then say: "If we stopped the webinar RIGHT here... just based on what I just showed you... you've probably already gotten more value than you get from even paid courses, yes? But we're just getting started! Wait until you see what I'm about to show you now..."

Each of trial closes is designed to get a micro-yes. Then there is a macro-YES, which is the BUY stage when the webinar participant clicks to order or takes the desired action.

Remove risk and barriers to the purchase. Give 30-day (or longer) money back "no questions asked" guarantees. The guarantee is particularly important for big-ticket purchases, especially if the webinar participant has a wife or husband that did not go through the webinar at the same time. These guarantees help remove high-price sticker-shock and can be followed up with customer service webinars to eliminate buyer remorse and build rapport.

Keep participants engaged by defying expectations. Cleverly say it wrong intentionally so that the usual becomes unusual. Can you turn your weakness into a strength?

Be prepared to answer real or perceived objections in your presentation. For example, if high price may be a concern, respond "When you invest in our program, imagine your Return on Investment and next thing you know you'll be telling the stories of your great results at the next cocktail party."

PITCH EXAMPLES

Your close is where you make your offer. Your offer may consist of:

- Physical product
- Digital product
- Service, such as consulting or coaching
- Membership program
- Application to go through a selection process
- Additional webinars with paid training

When you went through the WAMO Approach, you defined your desired outcome. Part of that outcome is your offer. The explanation of your offer can include:

- Description and images of what they get.
- What proof factors support the offer.
- What benefits they can enjoy with your offer components.
- What they pay and why it's a bargain.
- Why they risk nothing to get it (i.e., guarantee).
- Why they should act immediately to get it (bonuses, limited time or quantity).
- How to purchase your offer (web link, phone call, other).

Always remember this, people buy your offer not your product. Jon Schumacher says, "If your offer sucks, the greatest presentation in the world won't fix that."

Make an offer that gets your participants excited.

Your course or program or coaching has to be articulated in a way that has a clear benefit.

The bonuses must be very compelling and help fill in gaps or augment your core program. Don't add things just to add them. Make each aspect of your offer meaningful and exciting.

For example, if you have a course on Facebook advertising, you can include swipe file templates and email templates so people know how to write the copy for their ads.

On your webinar, you simply come right out and say you are going to offer all the participants something, and you frame it in such a way that they know it's in their best interest to see what your offer is. Your pacing should be fast with a lot of energy.

Spend an equal amount of time practicing your pitch. The Content and Connection all lead up to the Close. Become a master of the sequence of your closing slides, so that you can do it without looking. The more familiar you are with your close, the more effective your offer.

Pitch With A Diabolical Decoy

You may have one choice in your offer. You may have different payment options. You may have different "packages" or bundles. You can provide choice and contrast, but not too many options. Dan Ariely, the author of *Predictably Irrational*, conducted an experiment. If you were considering subscribing to *The Economist*, which offer would you prefer?

- Web Only $59
- Print and Web $125

Given the two choices, only a minority — 32% — opted for Print and Web (the desired outcome). Then a decoy was added.

- Web Only $59
- Print Only $125
- Print and Web $125

The decoy (Print Only for $125) is such a bad deal, you might think it was a mistake. No one took the decoy, Print Only. Why would anyone choose Print Only when they can get Print and Web for the same price? The decoy is there for the solely to make the Print and Web look like a good deal. The offerings were exactly the same.

The decoy, this one simple addition with nothing else changing, improved the percentage of respondents from 32% to 84% who chose Print and Web. (This was actually an ad that *The Economist* had used in an online advertisement; Ariely modified it to test the importance of the decoy.)

By adding an intentionally bad option as a decoy, you can make a product appear not only better than the decoy, but better overall. Used properly, this is one of the most diabolically effective presentation pitches.

The idea is to make one of the offers a "no brainer" decision. Look at the close section of your webinar and see if using a decoy in the offer will provide contrast. The decoy must fit in with your offer and make sense to your webinar participants.

STACKING YOUR OFFER

Stacking is when you stack both the offer and stack the close. You are quickly displaying the product offer images, supporting text, bonuses, and buy now button graphics, in rapid succession to create the value visually. Verbally you can stack multiple closes, one after another, each with a slightly different twist.

Use the Pitch Close statements before and after the product description and images of what they'll get when they purchase, and this must match the sales page offer.

Give a rationale for making the offer

Similar to a sales letter offer, the close or pitch on your webinar summarizes and answers questions about the major benefits your client gets from your product and what makes doing business with you "unique." The offer hits the target market's "hot buttons" and makes the webinar participant want to buy.

Spend some time on why you are making this offer. Give your webinar participants some logical reasoning why you are doing this. For example: you want to share what you've learned to make a positive impact on other people's lives. You could also tell them that you're tired of only the big guru players getting all the results. It should be a limited time offer. This rationale also acts as a transition from the content to get your webinar participants in the right frame of mind.

Make sure your website has a different page and order form for the "webinar only" offer. You could use a promo code for the discount, but that is an additional step. Remove obstacles and make it easy to buy. If they go to the "regular sales page," the price should be higher. After the time frame you defined is expired, redirect the "webinar only" page to the "regular sales page." Stay in integrity with your words.

Carefully and completely explain each component

Go through each component of your offer. Spend sufficient time on each to fully explain the following. Also be sure to use a "killer" graphic designed for each part of your offer. It may take a few slides to describe each component completely.

- What does this component do?
- What is included?
- What are all the features?
- What are the benefits?

You can "stack" the components in a list to demonstrate the value offered.

Using Scarcity

I highly recommend using scarcity with every offer you provide. Why? Scarcity will dramatically boost your conversion rate. After all, why would someone want to purchase if they can just come back next week to buy the same product? In reality, they never come back next week. Even if they do return, their emotional radar is at a lower level and they have forgotten the benefits of your offer.

SCARCITY TACTICS:

Limited time

Tell your webinar participants that the offer is only good for a limited number of hours or days. Make good on this promise so they know you are for real. If the offer is a big ticket item, you may want to give 1-2 days to allow them to check their bank accounts.

Bonuses will expire

It's wise to use bonuses as part of your offer. They make the attendee feel special. There's nothing more aggravating than having something important taken away, especially if it has high perceived value. You can have the bonuses expire in a few hours or, more commonly used, at midnight. This way your basic offer remains intact, it's simply the bonuses that are removed.

Limit the total number of products sold

If you are only selling a specific quantity at the introductory or special price, you can add this quantity to the sales pages as well as announce it on the webinar.

This scarcity method can be used to limit special bonuses. You tell them key bonuses are only good for a specific number—say, the first five customers. After this, the bonus goes away. You will need to give them a logical reason for limiting the offer. You can tell them that you only will be giving away five consultation spots due to time availability; you want to limit the market exposure for your product or just to reward the fast-action takers.

You can provide a countdown timer on your sales page, or by simply writing on the slides with annotations or a writing tablet. On the slide, be sure to write the numbers with a strikethrough, showing how many are left. You will probably need a second monitor to do this. Keep it honest and remove the bonus after you've reached your sales goal.

Listen to *The Webinar Way* interview with Greg Jacobs who has the nickname *The Best Webinar Pitchman.*

Price increase after 24-48 hours or quantities sold

Another common scarcity tactic is to raise the offer price after 24-48 hours, "X" number of days, or on a certain date. Also, a price increase after every ten products sold is a tactic used to encourage customers "to buy now" at the lowest price.

You will need to switch out the sales page after the given time or target quantity sold has been reached to change the price on the offer page and also your sales system.

PITCH: Clarity Trumps Persuasion

> ***"Everyone hears only what he understands."***
>
> *- Goethe*

Eliminate any confusion. Flint McGlaughlin says *"Clarity Trumps Persuasion."* It starts with the clear intention of your webinar invitation. Guide the thought process of your webinar guests to one conclusion: the point of action, which is to take you up on your offer.

If you care about your audience, take the time to clarify your message and make it concise. You want to convey ideas that are effortless to recall. Keep F.A.M.E. in mind.

If they can't repeat it, they didn't get it. Don't let that happen.

The journey is both aural and visual. Storyboard the images and integrate your "speech" for a cohesive message. You want people to remember, repeat and share your message.

Point out the value of each component

Discuss what each component means to your webinar participants and illustrate financial value. List the true monetary value beside the component image and text. Talk about the value to make an impact. You are stacking the total value of all the components in preparation for your closing, your final offer. Include your guarantee.

Summarize the offer

The offer needs to match the sales page, so use the same look and feel to maintain consistency. There are a couple of methods to summarize the offer. I suggest you use both. Go over each and discuss the component and its major benefit.

- Create a graphical collection of all the components onto one slide. Create smaller graphics for each component. Place a description below each graphic.
- Create a table listing each component. Next to the title of each, list the monetary value at the bottom, and tally the total value. You can use large size font or color accents to make the total value conspicuous.

Conduct a pricing countdown sequence

The countdown is optional. Many webinars do not show price at all but just discuss the components. Some only see the price when they get to the order page link with the buy button because this creates an added curiosity feature.

For the price countdown, the offer starts out at a very high initial price and then, step by step, the price is reduced, often with a strikethrough, until the final number is displayed.

It's important to take this pricing sequence one step at a time. Place each component and price on a separate slide and discuss why it's worth this amount of money. Or use a strikethrough through one price as the next price is displayed. The strikethrough on price shows what a deal they are getting on the webinar. Review the benefits and discuss in detail why they would be crazy not to take the offer at this price.

Give a reason for why you aren't asking for this higher price. For example: poor economy, special price for a particular group, looking for some partners who are motivated and will go through the program, or any reason that is true and makes sense.

When you get to the final price, use a separate slide. Highlight in a larger font and spend some time discussing why it's worth this amount.

If you offer a payment plan, then clearly state the terms here. If you have a no-risk, money-back guarantee, provide the details. You'll find that the combination of a payment plan and also a guarantee will dramatically boost your sales conversions.

Provide a web link to sales offer page

At the end of your close, you want them to click on your offer page link to process the order.

This offer page should use a URL that is easy to type or remember. It may be advantageous to use the same root domain in a webinar series to maintain familiarity, or to track joint venture partner links. Example: **http://webinarwelove.com/go**

The sales offer page only needs to restate the offer as explained on the webinar. Show the graphics, list each component of the offer and include an attractive BUY button.

If you have a payment plan or a guarantee, show this on the offer page in the form of a seal or guarantee certificate. Match it with your webinar content.

On the sales page, to be compliant, add your links for: privacy policy, disclaimer or terms & conditions. Please consult a professional for legal advice for where to display these important announcements. These links are also critical for advertising approvals.

PITCH CLOSING STATEMENTS

Listen to *The Webinar Way* interview with Athena Davis as she describes many of the close types she experienced as a webinar participant.

Some (much more in the Power of Webinars training program) closing statements you can "stack" together, or just choose one:

- "You'll forget everything" close — "Bridging the gap between new information and implementation. HUGE gap! Some of you on this webinar think that you 'got it'… but psychologists tell us you don't…" "48 hours from now you'll have forgotten everything I talked about and half of what you thought as a result of what I talked about, and 16 days from now you won't remember having been on this webinar let alone what we discussed today…"
- The Strategy Session close — Popular with coaches and consultants, the offer of a strategy session, free consultation, discovery call or similar name keeps the conversation going after the webinar is over. See more in Follow-Up in a couple pages.
- "I'll sleep well tonight, will you?" close — "Whether or not you say yes to this wonderful opportunity today, I'll still sleep well tonight. Fact is, my life will still be great. I'll [insert what you'll enjoy and what your life is like because you've already achieved the solution they desperately want...] "So I'll sleep well tonight. But will you? Will you be able to sleep knowing that you could've done something to change your future?… To change what you're currently getting into something more? To take a step closer to [insert ideal solution they want]. Will

you be able to sleep if you let this opportunity pass you by? … "Especially when, if you act right now, you get these special fast action bonuses… [insert bonuses] I think the choice is clear. Join me now."

- The Live Testimonial close — Surprise Guest. Someone who has purchased and is willing to jump on the webinar and say how it has changed their life or improved their situation. This testimonial is usually planned in advance.
- "Add one more thing" close — Before the webinar, you deliberately hold back a special, attractive bonus or part of the offer that you will "intentionally" forget to mention until right before the webinar ends, and after you've gone through details of your offer. (This can be listed as a special unannounced bonus on your sales page.)
- The "access to authority" close — Only through membership/purchase (if it applies).
- The "other possibility" close – "In the time we had today, I have given you the tools to take action to get results. And, if this was your only option, it would be satisfactory. But what if there WAS another possibility? An option that allows us to do this together? I'd like to introduce…"
- The "any reason" close – "Is there any reason you wouldn't take us up on our offer today?" (ask question to get feedback to overcome objections)
- The "webinar price only" close — You make your offer at the end only good until the webinar is over. Then the price increases and you remove a bonus. (You must automate the update or have a separate sales page with a different price ready to swap out with a new link.)

- The Q & A close — After you've done your first close or two, you ease up from the "official closes" and start answering questions. Listen to Tony Laidig and Brian Bagnall discuss how they use the Q&A close in their interviews.
- "Get off this webinar now" close — (as part of the Q&A) – "We're about to finish up this webinar. If you invested in the special offer I made, please stay on the webinar. Everyone else who didn't invest, please sign off right now – I'll give you a minute… thank you for attending, but I want to talk to those now who signed up and answer their questions…" State that "the Q&A is only for people who purchase." Make it sound exclusive. Now start speaking with NEW OWNERS of your product.

If you've done an excellent job with the 3Cs, providing great content, connecting with webinar participants and closing, you will see the sales start ringing up. Cha-ching!

The last of the Five UPs is follow-up. You continue to follow-up after the webinar through email and other methods of connection. If you have offered a strategy session, then you connect on the phone or through Skype or Zoom. During this follow-up you can use a set of questions similar to these to further the sale: *Was there anything that really stood out for you during the presentation? How does your business work? What's your biggest challenge? What's your big WHY for being in your business? How do you think we may be able to help you? Do you have a budget for this? Would you like to hear a few ways (options) we can help you?*

Continue to follow-up, provide value and build relationships.

If this is your first pilot webinar, you will be elated and exhausted. Pat yourself on the back for accomplishing your first Payday Webinar!

If this is your 100th webinar, you'll be plugging your numbers into *The Webinar Way Profit Calculator* to check on your performance and profits.

Congratulations!

The Role of a Webinar Host During The Pitch

We'll be talking about PARTNERS in the next pillar. The role of a Joint Venture Partner (JVP) or webinar host during the pitch can be a key transition point before the close. Their credibility makes it all the more compelling.

Simply have the JVP or webinar host ask this question at the appropriate time:

"Can you tell us how we can get a copy of this?" or

"Can you tell us how we can get access to this?" or

"Can you tell us how we can get more of this?"

This page intentionally left blank

PILLAR 7: PARTNER

> ***"Joint ventures between two companies for the benefit of their customers represents the greatest opportunity for upside profit potential."***
>
> *- Mark Hendricks,*
> *The Grandmaster of Joint Ventures*

Joint Ventures, Other People's Products

- **Joint Ventures:** Will your webinar offer benefit another company's customer base? Can yòu turn your competitors into partners?
- **Other People's Products:** How do you promote and profit from another company's product to license, present, and offer it on a webinar?

One of the most important reasons to partner is because your customers and prospects will tire of the same presenters and points of views. Offering new webinar topics, exciting presenters with unique expertise, product, insights and perspectives keeps things fresh for your audience.

Of the four categories of webinar profit models, the first is your products and services and the next three can involve partners.

- Your Product/Service (product owner)
- Other People's Product/Service (As affiliate or representative)
- Joint Venture Webinars & Summits
- Automated Webinars (We discuss this in *The Webinar Lifestyle* section of the book)

We will start the Partner discussion about becoming a JPV (Joint Venture Partner) as a product owner who is looking for a JVP list owner.

What is a Joint Venture?

A joint venture is simply when two businesses agree to promote the products or services of one business to the customers of the other business. One company provides the product and the other company provides this list of customers.

As a product owner, in launching a new webinar advertising campaign to a cold market, you can spend some serious money to pay a sales letter copywriter, crafting the offer, creating the follow-up sequences, split testing and see (perhaps) a 1-3% conversion rate (assuming you do everything properly).

An alternative is to execute a joint venture to grow your business. Joint ventures are the ultimate form of leverage. To propel the awesome financial power of joint ventures, combine several forms of leverage: OPR (other people's resources) and OPC (other people's customers). You want to find a great JVP list owner.

The first business gets introduced to the buying customers of the second business who knows, likes, and trusts the second business. With the rapport and existing relationship with the second business, these customers are more willing to purchase because of the endorsement of the first business by the second business.

Both businesses profit from the relationship and the customers do too. It's a great example of Relationship Riches and a win-win-win for all involved.

Let's say you have a product or service that sells well, but you'd like to increase your customer base quickly. You contact another company who already has the type of customers you want, and set up a deal with them and agree to run a webinar. The JVP list owner is in fact endorsing you, your company and your product to their list.

The JVP List Owner promotes your product to their list of customers, and you provide them an attractive offer on your webinar. You, like the JVP Product Owner, can either split the costs of the distribution of your offer to their list of customers (by mail, email, or telemarketing, PPCs, social media, etc.), or you agree to pay the costs upfront and deduct costs from the profits, before splitting the revenue with your joint venture partner on the resulting sales. Everything is negotiable.

You acquire lots of new and profitable customers very quickly, and your JVP harvests profits that are hidden in their business, because the offer on the webinar is a new revenue stream for a product of interest to your customers.

You get more and more sales from these newly acquired customers for years to come, and your JVP reaps more profits from the time and expense of building their customer base.

PARTNER: JOINT VENTURE WEBINAR

Webinars happen to be the medium that most joint ventures are looking to promote. Why? Because there are numbers to back up your previous success and there are immediate sales that follow.

Several of *The Webinar Way* interviews are with Joint Venture Webinar Brokers such as Willie Crawford, Sohail Kahn, Muhammad Siddique, Seth Larrabee, Christina Vendley and others. It is not easy work; some have left and others, like Sohail, have gone on to write a book on joint ventures.

The art of the joint venture is its own business, and both Willie Crawford and Sohail Kahn offer in-depth training in this arena.

Once your webinar educational content has been proven, you can offer it to strategic partners and create a joint venture. This JV may lead to guest appearances on their webinars or you can develop a webinar collaboration. Joint Ventures help increase your referrals, grow your list and eventually lead to more business. Developed relationships with numerous people inside and outside your industry to build your client base and expand more referrals that provide exposure, reach new audiences, and increase your network.

If you need more leads and clients, the key question to ask yourself is: *"Where do my ideal customers/clients go for business BEFORE they do business with me?"*

Consider the two roles of JVP Product Owner and JVP List Owner:

As the JVP Product Owner, plan out the joint venture opportunity by identifying the benefits to the list partner about YOUR product or service. Offer massive value for the list company. Think about all the benefits that you bring to the table. The JVP List Owner will want to know why your product is a good fit for their list of customers. They will want to know how your webinar converts, EPC (earnings per click), what bonuses you are offering, etc.

The JVP List Owner may have a JV Questionnaire that you will need complete to see if you qualify. If your product/service is a good fit, the list partner will gladly promote you and your company to their customers! You will split the profits after the webinar.

This partial list of questions is from Sohail Khan about selecting a JVP.

7 Important Questions You MUST Ask Potential JV Partners

1. **Is your mailing list composed of buyers or visitors/leads?** Buyers have always been and will always be more profitable than leads. Knowing if there are some visitors in that list is VERY important, as they have been known to complain about spam/junk mail, even if they signed-up to receive future mailings.
2. **How big is your mailing list?** If they don't have enough names, forget it. As a rule of thumb, bigger is better. However, if you are selling a high-ticket product, then this is not always the case.

3. **How often do you contact your mailing list?** Monthly to weekly contact is excellent. But anything more often than that may hinder your chances of reaching the maximum percentage of prospects possible.
4. **Do customers buy from you often and, if so, how often on average?** The more they buy, the better, because they are used to spending money with the owner of the list. Customers that buy often from or follow the recommendation of a list owner is a very good sign, because you know that they have a good relationship. Tap into those *Relationship Riches.*
5. **What is the percentage of clients who bought more than once from you?** Knowing the percentage of repeat buyers is important, as it will give you a very good idea of the relationship they do or don't have with the list owner and, also, if the potential JV partner is a savvy marketer who has the customer's best interest in mind.
6. **How much did customers pay per product, on average, in the past?** If your product or service is priced along those lines, that's great. If not, you have the choice of lowering your price just for that one deal or dropping the deal altogether.
7. **Does the JVP conduct webinars on a regular basis to their list?** If so, does that mean their list is fatigued or excited when they hear about a new webinar? Can you choose the timing of your webinar presentation so it does not conflict with other promotions?

Joint ventures can skyrocket your authority and your wealth. In any business, being able to leverage somebody else's database of prospects and customers and springboard off another person's credibility puts you in a position to generate vast amounts of cash flow as a result. In the joint venture agreement, you sell your product to someone else's database and often it is an even 50/50 split of the profits.

Joint ventures are significant because you don't need your own customer list, product, your own website or your own traffic.

The key here is to identify people, companies, and prospective joint venture partner companies who have a list, a product and a website, but they're not doing webinars. There are databases of people, both prospects and customers. Perhaps they don't have any idea how to do webinars. You can take the webinar process, apply it to their business and help them sell more products. You'll be seen as the hero because you help generate sales in a channel they did not have access to previously.

You can help your JVP using experts to help sell more products and services to more people using things they already have in place.

How to Find JVPs

Of course, asking, networking and meeting face to face is one way to get referrals for your JVPs. But another way is to look at the live events listed on Eventbrite and MeetUp. Those events have organizers and those organizers are attracting your target audience. You'll have to wait until after their live event to run the webinar but it is a great way to provide those who did not attend to get the value you'll deliver on your next webinar. The event organizers are waiting for you! Put a proposal together to show you mean business.

JVPs: A Word about Contact Information and Affiliate Links

Joint venture webinar presentations differ from your presentation because of the "contact ability." On your handouts, bonus PDFs, slides, website, etc., you want to include contact information for your website, customer service, social media links, blog, etc. When you are conducting a joint venture, most often the partner who is "bringing the list" will want you to remove your contact information. This link uniqueness requirement is because the JVP wants the focus to be on one web link that ties to their commission. Since the JVP customers are introduced to you, the JVP wants to benefit financially by having their customer purchase from an offer link (URL is unique resource locator domain link) that ties directly to their commission.

The offer link is basically an affiliate link. You will need to set up your own affiliate program. You can simply generate affiliate links or build out a full affiliate resource website containing:

- Link Generator, Banner Ads, Buttons, Graphics, Videos, FAQs, instruction and tips

As mentioned in Pillar 6 PITCH, at the end of your close, the webinar participants will be directed to click over to your offer link to process the order.

This offer link should use a URL that is easy to type or remember. It may be advantageous to use the same root domain for all JVPs and use their name in the link. Examples:

http://webinarwelove.com/**jim**

http://webinarwelove.com/**susan**

http://webinarwelove.com/**casey**

Joint Venture Partners may want to use their unique domain URL for the order link on the webinar.

Be prepared to create customized announcement emails for your JVP and at least four promo emails. If you have created a full-fledged affiliate program, encourage your affiliates to enter the email sequence you create for their customers in their email auto-responder.

Joint Venture Webinars can:

- Make you huge profits very fast
- Give you instant credibility in markets you want to access
- Build your list of customer and prospect databases quickly
- Create profitable business relationships that can last for years
- Help you harvest profits from your customer base that you could not access yourself

CASE STUDY: A webinar was a key feature as part of the roll-out of a product called the App Code, a training program capitalizing on the trend of mobile apps that teaches people how to build high-demand iPhone and Android Apps. This product is no longer available as the marketplace changed quickly. It was run as live and automated sales webinars.

The joint venture partners who hosted live webinars for The App Code, and who had responsive lists, were paid handsomely. Some of the joint venture partners' earnings were reported for the webinar:

Trey Smith earned $328 per attendee, Gauher Chaudhry earned $205 per attendee, and Dax Aurand made $326 per attendee.

CASE STUDY: Minesh Bhindi who is the founder of http://www.goldandsilverforlife.com says "Wealth exclusively equals the power to create. I can't tell you how to use that power, but I know we can help you keep it in economic cycles when the vultures are circling."

His webinar: "3 Steps To Cash-Flow Gold & Silver For A Passive Income Of 12% - 26.4% Per Year Just Like Real Estate!" has had excellent net EPC earnings:

Donny Gamble earned $39 per click, Michael Wilding earned $11 per click, and Andy Shaw made $32 per click.

If you're interested in the subject of this webinar, you can contact Rakhee who manages the strategic partnerships for Minesh. They are based in London, UK.

HOW DO JOINT VENTURES WORK?

There are two types of joint venture deals:

- Complementary
- Competitive

Many joint ventures are set up with complementary (non-competing) businesses who share the same type of customers. With a well-structured joint venture agreement, you can even set up JV webinars with your competition because this can benefit both you, your competitor and your customers. This is sometimes called "co-opetition."

Even direct competitors conduct joint ventures because they know that, ultimately, if there is an opportunity for a sale and a competitor's product offers what the prospective customer is looking for, they would rather get a percentage of the sale than nothing at all. Also, competitors in the same marketplace know many customers buy from multiple product owners.

You either find your own JV deals or work with a JV Webinar Broker. JV Webinar Brokers take a percentage of the profits, anywhere from 10% to 25%, to find you webinar JV opportunities.

Whether you set up Joint Ventures for yourself or have someone do it for you, you'll want to add joint venture webinars into your marketing mix.

JOINT VENTURE WEBINAR ACTIVITIES

In most cases, before a JV deal is struck, you will share your webinar metrics based on past experience from your own webinar performance or other JVs you've done. You will have a set or negotiable profit-sharing arrangement.

- They will endorse you and your product to their customer list.
- You will provide them a sample of your product or service first so they can experience the quality of your products and services, and they will be comfortable based on personal experience to endorse you to their customers.
- Define who will write all the emails and letters (often with the editorial approval of the other party), and whether or not you split the marketing cost. Or you may offer to pay all expenses for the distribution of the offer (after all, you are leveraging off the goodwill your joint venture partner has built over the years with their

customers so you can gain instant access to new paying customers for your business).

Remember, a webinar is an event. One or more of the "players" in a webinar event coordinates many activities to make the webinar event a success.

E. Brian Rose (no relation to Sherrie Rose) was approached by James Jones to take his $27 product, create a webinar, and sell the training for the product for $199. James had a responsive audience for Brian's subject and sold 300 units. Sales of almost $60,000 on Brian's first JVP webinar got him hooked on webinars and partnering, and he started Webinar Swaps.

Sherrie met Mark Anastasi at Armand Morin's Persuasion X Speaker Training. Mark is the author of *Laptop Millionaire*, and he says, "I made over $200,000 in 90 minutes on my first ever webinar." It was joint venture webinar and the product cost $1,000. His results are not typical, because he started with his own **huge customer base to promote to and 1,000 people registered.** He was well-established and had the right connections, and he also paid to get additional exposure with solo ads to targeted prospect lists and 1,200 more people registered. Over 700 people watched the webinar event live.

We don't have EPC (earnings per click data) or replay data but, using *The Webinar Way Profit Calculator,* here are some important numbers on Mark's joint venture webinar:

Live Participant Rate: 31.25%

Sales Closing Rate: 28.57%

Earnings per Registrant: $ 89.29

Earnings per Live Participant: $ 285.71

Mark split the earnings 50/50 with the webinar presenter. Splitting $200,000 is a very nice payday for a 90 minute webinar event. Of course, this does not include planning time and preparation but, however you look at it, *Webinars Rock!*

PARTNER: PROMOTE AND PROFIT FROM OTHER PEOPLE'S PRODUCTS

Partnering can take on many forms and can be a very creative process. Include joint venture webinars às an active part of the overall marketing plan for your business. Here are eight ideas for partnering using other people's products and webinars.

1. Licensing Other People's Webinars

License the webinar and corresponding sales materials. Matt Lloyd had a set of webinars he used for promotion, but was missing one that would round it out. He contacted Jonathan Budd who had a successful automated webinar. He licensed the sales materials and webinar and added it to his marketing mix.

2. Translating a Webinar

Partner with someone and translate their webinar and license it. Their webinar may have great visuals and a great script. If they provide a consulting service that is beneficial to consultants in the same field, but who have clients speaking different languages, then the slides and script can be translated and licensed. This also works for your own webinar, which can be translated and licensed.

Represent other people's product/service. You present and represent other people's products on a webinar. These webinars can be for lead generation and to promote other people's product or service for a commission.

- **Local Business Webinars** (lead generation, service offer)
- **Affiliate Marketing Webinar** (other people's product/service)
- **Network Marketing Webinar** (other people's product/service)
- **Interview Style Webinar** (other people's product/service)
- **Joint Venture Webinars and Summits**
- **Joint Venture Automated Webinar Offerings**

3. Local Business Webinars

Your client is your partner. As a consultant, you conduct webinars on behalf of your local client. This could be a retail business, professional, service provider, etc. You do this to educate your client's customer and drive leads with some sort of incentive. This is taking offline to online and back to offline.

You conduct webinars to attract local business clients. This is a lead generation technique to educate prospects. The close is often a complementary strategy session. The strategy session close is also popular with coaches and consultants.

4. Affiliate Marketing Webinar

Your affiliate product is your partner. Instead of sending your prospects to a sales page, you conduct your own webinar, describing the benefits of the product. Brittany Lynch suggests taking the sales page for an affiliate product and using these as the teaching points. Use the Persuasion Map (one of your bonuses when you signed up) to create your main teaching points. If you need assistance, then claim your free webinar strategy session: http://thewebinarway.com/claimit

5. Network Marketing Webinar

Your MLM product is your partner. Joel Peterson and David Frey are successful in the company called Send Out Cards, which is a Network Marketing organization. They promote via webinars. They train their MLM (multi-level marketing) distributor downline via webinars. Check the rules defined by the organization that you need to follow with regards to marketing.

6. Interview Style Webinar

Turn to your interview skills and get other experts to be the "star" of your webinar. Steve Essa made $18,000 in sales in a joint venture, interview-style webinar, on a $3000 product. Emails went out to 1,000 people; 60 people attended live and 10% purchased.

Perhaps you've seen someone speak on stage and they have a great product to sell. If they have a presentation that can be easily modified for a webinar, you're almost ready to go.

If they don't have a prepared presentation, you can ask for the key points and prepare the presentation slides so there is a visual element. Slides must have a strong visual impact or you are better off conducting a tele-seminar. You will have the key talking points and can switch slides as the interview progresses. Then the expert just has to talk. Practice the presentation because 'practice makes profit.'

You set up the webinar platform and you are the webinar host. You interview with engaging questions. You can now partner with people all over the world.

At the same time, you're building huge creditability with your webinar participants by bringing in experts. You're building your own network of experts and you're allowing everybody into your business to see what you're doing, what you're learning, and you're sharing in the profits with that expert.

This is similar to a joint venture, but you will have a prepared set of questions for the guest expert. It is as if the participants are eavesdropping on your conversation. A great "prize" is to open up the lines and have a Q&A session at the end so the webinar participants can ask questions.

7. Joint Venture Webinar & Summits

You are a webinar joint venture broker or you have JV brokers find matching customer lists or related products for your customers. Webinar JV brokers find, secure, license, and establish JV Partnerships. Joint ventures are also used in single-day or multi-day Webinar Summits. These webinars can become the basis for a membership site.

8. Joint Venture Automated Webinar Systems

You have a high converting webinar and set it up on "auto-pilot." You can also license other people's webinars and include them in your marketing funnel. You can promote a joint venture webinar with an automated system. More about automated webinars in the section of this book called *The Webinar Lifestyle.*

POINTERS FOR PROFITABLE JV PARTNERSHIPS

> ***"The Real Currency Is Relationship Riches."***
>
> *- Sherrie Rose*

Dustin Matthews is in the speaker training business with Dave VanHoose. You can see their videos on *The Webinar Way* YouTube Channel. Together they run 7 Figure Speaking Empire, and they recommend automating your webinar. Dustin offers these five solid pointers that will dramatically increase your odds of launching a profitable JV partnership:

Don't take it personally. Sought-after JVPs are busy folks. Remember: we all experience a certain amount of "Nos" to get to the "Yeses," so don't take it personally. Don't react. Never fire back an angry email. Keep your professional reputation intact — you never know when you might have an opportunity to cross that same bridge, or one that's connected to it, in the future.

Add your personal touch. Most partner-worthy JVPs are bombarded with daily requests, so they can smell a template a mile away. Sure, templates can save you time in the short run, but they could also cost you everything. Think about it: would you respond to someone who approached you with a message that started with "Dear Website Owner?" Hand-craft your communications, and the more details you can include showing you've done your homework the better. Plus, be sure to refer to the recipient by name.

Give before you receive. According to Stephen Covey, we need to learn to manage the "emotional bank accounts" for our relationships — not just with family, but also friends and people we work with, including JVPs. This account represents the level of trust and confidence you have with others. Every account starts at a neutral level, strengthens as you make deposits (things like showing personal integrity and keeping commitments), and weakens when you make withdrawals (like asking for favors). The key is to make far more deposits so you'll still be in a positive position when you make mistakes, which you'll inevitably do since you're human. The most common mistake people make when approaching potential JVPs is to ask for something right out of the gate. Don't think because you have a great solution that'll make them a boatload of money that you're starting out on equal footing. Make no mistake—you're asking for a favor with an empty bank. Prove yourself before you prove your solution, and never ask them for something before you've done just that.

Friendship first. It's not enough to just tell people you're trustworthy and credible. They have to experience it for themselves. The best way to demonstrate these assets, along with your other irresistible qualities, is to let them get to know you first. Especially if you're just starting out and trying to make a name for yourself, you need to prove to them you're someone they need to do business with. That process starts with friendship. Personal time together establishes a personal connection. Listening to and understanding what's important to another are two ways to make huge deposits in your account. And there's no better place to start making initial deposits than at events. They give you the time and opportunity to get to know potential JVPs, find out what motivates them and what they're working on. Mari Smith, who wrote the foreword for this book, says, "Relationship first."

Leverage the Law of Reciprocity: How do you feel when someone does you a favor then, a week later, asks you to do something for them? Chances are the idea of not returning the favor is emotionally painful and goes against your core values of right and wrong. As human beings, we feel obligated to help people who help us—reciprocity is a HUGE motivator. So how does this apply to JVPs? The fastest way to get a potential partner's attention is to promote their product and make them a ton of money first. But what if you have no list and that's not an option? There are plenty of other ways to build goodwill. What about connecting them to someone you know who could benefit them in some way? Or once you have a clear picture of what they're working on, pass on a relevant article or news item that could help them in their cause? If you come at it with a "What can I do for you?" mindset, you'll find ways to demonstrate you genuinely care about helping others get results.

Finding the right JVP can explode your business faster than every other strategy combined. No doubt, the thought of approaching a potential JVP is a bit scary at first but, by putting these five relationship-building skills into practice, you're guaranteed to get amazing results.

You can also share profits with a JV webinar broker. In Pillar 1, Perspective, we talked about the parts or roles you can perform in a webinar. One of those roles is a webinar profit coordinator or webinar broker. There is a lot of work involved in putting on a webinar event, so it's a smart move to engage a webinar broker who will bring more opportunities your way.

Tips To Effectively Connect With An Influencer

There are big and small influencers who can quickly turn into strategic partners and eventually joint venture partners for your webinar and your business. Harry Kraus compiled this list to help connect with influencers in your market.

Step 1: Write down top hot keywords that are commonly used in your industry that influencers often talk about

Step 2: Go to Buzzsumo.com and type in those keywords.

Step 3: Open articles that are most relevant to your audience with a high amount of exposure and write down a list of the influencers.

Step 4: Find their social media pages, connect with them on all platforms… Facebook, LinkedIn, Instagram, YouTube, Twitter, Snapchat

Step 5: Write a personalized message complementing or providing value to them.

Step 6: Build a relationship by reaching out and providing value to them at the same time. Find out what they value in their business, what is their biggest pain point, what they are looking for to help their idea of growth. Keep mental reminders to be sure what you are proposing in the future aligns with their vision of success.

Step 7: After 5-6 touch points or after a relationship has been established privately message them with a partnership opportunity. The partnership has to be in alignment with how they determine if someone is a valuable strategic partner…

Step 8: Take Action and Make It Happen!

PRO-TIP: Use Nimble to develop rapport and connect with influencers. Nimble.com is a CRM that works wherever you're engaging prospective customers and clients. The Nimble Smart Contacts App provides the context you need to connect intelligently and take action from any social site or business app.

## PART IV

THE WEBINAR LIFESTYLE

The Webinar Lifestyle

You've seen the headlines:

How to Quit Your Job and Make a Good Living on the Internet!

A Surprisingly Simple Way to Make Money Online...

Create positive change and achieve extraordinary results!

We can help you begin your journey as a coach.

Secrets Revealed: Create a Full-Time Income From home and Let Amazon do ALL of the Fulfillment for You!

Wouldn't it be great if you could work from anywhere and set your own schedule?

Of all the tactics and strategies on the Internet, webinars can bring you closer to the lifestyle you choose than any other. The RIGHT webinar, as part of your business strategy with the right market, can give you absolute freedom, and every morning you'll wake up, excited about the day ahead, and say to yourself, "I can't believe people pay me to do this!"

Some people want to split their time between living in their home city and travelling around the world. Others just want to be able to buy a few more luxuries. Many just want more time with their families and to be able to attend all their kids' activities, without asking for the boss for time off.

To live *The Webinar Lifestyle*, you begin by choosing to pursue a business around a lifestyle, instead of a lifestyle controlled by your business. This is the premise of Jim Kukral's 3-part book series, *Business Around A Lifestyle.*

You can build a business around the concepts in one excellent webinar presentation. A well-converting webinar is a BIG asset.

There is absolutely no reason you shouldn't have the life you've always wanted. Life is too short to live that way. Jim's book has stories and examples from the lifestyle entrepreneurs that will open your mind to this very true reality and, hopefully, get you to finally understand these facts.

Take a look around and you'll see that this shift to becoming a lifestyle entrepreneur is being adopted by more and more people every day. Some people are falling into it, because they have been laid off from their jobs and are literally forced into it. Some people just figure out a way to make it happen, because they want to take their life into their own hands.

You can catch a lucky break and have a well-known person with a huge list of potential webinar participants invite you to present and sell your product or service on a webinar. Most likely, you will have to prove your webinar and find joint venture partners or, better yet, have a webinar broker working for you, finding opportunities for you to present your webinar.

Many people who participate in high-end coaching mention webinars. Brian Price talks about his webinars with his mentor, how he is super passionate about everything he does, how he puts everything into his webinars and more.

Listen to Nick Peall's interview and how he re-oriented his business with webinars. Hands down, webinars are the most lucrative channel for profit.

Once you have your WAMO figured out, your 3C by 3T Matrix defined, and your 7 Pillars established, all you have to do is show up and give your webinar presentation.

Or do you?

PERPETUAL PROFITS – AUTOMATED WEBINARS

Perpetual profits can be created by implementing automation and perpetual launches for round-the-clock webinars.

Automated Webinars. We have hinted at automated webinars throughout *The Webinar Way*. If you don't even have to show up to give the webinar presentation, now that's the true *Webinar Lifestyle*!

There are a few things you need to put in place before you can "set it and forget it." First, you must have a tested, well-converting webinar. Listen to Brian Ridgway's interview on *The Webinar Way*. He ran his introductory webinar twice a week, for six months, before adding an automated webinar.

An automated webinar is often part of an 'evergreen launch' if the subject matter remains valid. Autopilot webinars are "perpetual webinars" that you set to play at a certain time and day of the week. Expect perpetual profits with a well-tested webinar.

Automated webinars are a fantastic tool because you can share your best converting webinar. The idea of a webinar is that it's an "event." An event requires attendance to get training and exposure to you and to your product or service.

When done right, automated webinars can be a great tool that leads to *The Webinar Lifestyle* you desire. Automate your high-converting webinars for perpetual profits.

In the Resource Section, links are provided to examples of automated webinars.

Perpetual Launch. Once your subscriber begins to receive your automated email responders, you invite them to a new product offering being released "next week." However, what they'll be viewing is a pre-recorded webinar event that will look and feel as if it's a brand new product launch. The best part is that it happens automatically without any additional involvement from you.

- NOTE: When recording, don't mention the time of day. Don't mention seasons or weather. Don't mention dates in the webinar. If you do at the start of the webinar, edit these out.

Around-the-clock Webinars. A webinar registration page identifies the time and date that a visitor registers. Based on the platform you are using, and how you set up the webinar options, the registration can select a date/time, right now, or an hour from now to watch the next webinar. These "just-in-time" on-demand webinars start within minutes of registration. This is an extremely powerful technique, which almost always guarantees you an audience, because interest is high. These on-demand webinars are basically videos but are placed on pages that have all the buttons and options to buy and submit questions.

Joint Venture Automated Webinars. Create a customized automated webinar for your JVP. Pre-record an introduction and exit with your JVP. Offer a unique bonus. Determine the timeframe for the automated webinar. Create a custom registration page, with photos of the presenter and the JVP.

AUTOMATED PLATFORM: There are three main choices for an automated webinar platform.

1. Feature Built into Your Live Webinar Platform
2. WordPress Plugin

3. Standalone System

Live Webinar Platform. Online recording: Have your recordings automatically saved online in your webinar platform. Your webinar recordings are automatically saved and from there you can view, download and share them with attendees. Note this is different than local recording when you have your recordings saved locally on your computer's hard drive.

WordPress Plugin. Many people have a blog and would like to keep their web traffic and activity on the same domain. If you are using WordPress for your blog, you can choose to publish to WordPress. Many of the WordPress plugins allow you to run webinars on your WordPress website and can organize live and automated webinars. These are usually customizable with Google Hangouts on Air for live webinars, or webinar recording video from Youtube or Vimeo. This means no FTP or help from a developer or programmer is required! With the unique video player, video upload has been made simple.

Dynamic options where webinar registrant can choose:

- Everyday
- Specific Date
- One Day a Week
- Selected Days in the Week

Delayed Event and Call-to-action Settings. Select multiple delayed events within the webinar video for greater interaction, with a media library of several different call-to-action buttons to choose from.

Email Notification system. Notifying your registrants can be quite a task. We have made it simple with our own customizable email notification system that will send out notifications to the registrants several times before the webinar begins.

Webinar Plugin Widget. This type of feature allows you to add a registration box to any site or Facebook fan page. There is a dynamic display of the list of attendees that sign up for the webinar event. It displays the registrant's name at the top of the list.

In-Real-Time Chat box feature. This allows registrants to ask questions while the webinar is going, then notifies you via email. You or a moderator can answer at the time of the webinar, or ideally within 24 hours.

Webinar Plugin Social Sharing Tool. On the Thank You page, after someone signs up to the webinar, you can create a call to action in order to "spread the word" of the event, by offering a free gift that can be unlocked by clicking "share."

Unit Scarcity Tool. This is one of Cialdini's persuasion weapons, scarcity. You can choose a time within the webinar where a call to action button will show how many units are available, with a countdown to zero.

Edit Published Webinar Events. What if you created a webinar event video, but then a week later decide you want to change it? Most webinar platforms make you start from scratch. Analytics and split testing are additional features.

Proof. Social proof with tools like useproof.com display recently verified attendee registrations. These are particularly good on the automated webinar registration page but also work on live registration pages. This improves conversions and gets more registrations. However, it is another distraction and your prospect may click the link and go to the UseProof page instead of signing up for the webinar.

You create Rolling Webinars that play on autopilot. To use the Smart-Date technology, you just set the days of the week and what time, or times, of the day it should play. The key is to offer both date and time as "separate" selections. So that means if you want to do four webinars a week and four times a day, you can. Your visitor first selects from one of four different days, and then selects again in another section from one of four different times.

Set "Black-Out Dates," like Christmas, and eliminate short-notices by choosing to block today, or a few days before they can see your webinar, to build anticipation prior to your webinar.

If you are working with affiliates, you can add a "hard-expire" feature that allows the affiliates to see the urgency through both emailing several times before the event and immediately emailing replays afterwards, especially when the webinar converted. This allows them to see instant results, which many affiliates like, and makes it easier for you to ask for replay mailings. This exclusive feature is very important.

You can host your webinars on your own domain, or you can host them on their servers… 100% free of charge! It is a one-time purchase for the Ever system, with no monthly fees.

EverWebinar's sister product, WebinarJam, includes live webinars using Google Hangouts on Air. The live and automated webinars are on the same platform and user interface. The hybrid webinars are recorded but the chat is live. Mike Filsaime says the 5 "laws" of a no- fail webinar are to:

- Increase registrations
- Increase show-up rate

- Increase stick rate through the webinar
- Increase sales conversions
- Echo through automation (he promotes EverWebinar)

EverWebinar also includes a course that is designed to make online business owners a top-level webinar expert in just a day's worth of training. Personally, I know it takes more than a day to create a mesmerizing webinar experience that participants love and buy.

For best results, we recommend running your webinar live several times before turning it into on-demand or hybrid webinar.

Standalone System: Stealth Seminar is the longest running automated webinar software available. Geoff Ronning and his team provide great tech support and is a solid platform for automated webinars and has scarcity and urgency built in.

Evergreen Business Systems has since been replaced by EverWebinar (same developer). If you want to set up multiple webinars, simply record your webinar one time and let the system do the rest. Tip: If you don't want the YouTube logo on your EverWebinar. use JamCast as your webinar provider.

Do you have an effective presentation that you can make available as an on-demand webinar?

Prospects can choose the date and time to consume webinars. Recordings of high-converting webinars can be made available within an automated sales funnel.

If you're nervous about hosting a live webinar, would a hybrid webinar reduce the pressure?

A hybrid webinar has both pre-recorded and live elements. This allows the presenter to respond to questions in the chat even without a moderator, while the pre-recorded presentation is playing.

Hybrid Webinars capabilities are offered in many webinar platforms and use a recorded webinar. While the webinar is running you engage with participants and answer questions in real time. If available, like WebinarNinja platform, you can jump on camera/webcam during the hybrid webinar.

There are tools to help with urgency on your automated webinars. DeadlineFunnel.com creates evergreen deadlines for your leads and gives prospects a reason to take action now.

Claim Your Webinar Strategy Session & Start Your Own Perpetual Profit System

INVITATION: Free Webinar Strategy Session

Go to: http://thewebinarway.com/claimit

All owners of the book *The Webinar Way* are eligible for a one-time short consultation session. Get the details of your webinar strategy session for your very first pilot webinar, or learn how to uncover more profits from an existing webinar.

TRAINING: The Power of Webinars

Go to: http://PowerofWebinars.com

The Power of Webinars is an online training program developed as a turn-key approach, completely systematized and ready to go so you can get up and running fast! This is a paid program.

Webinars are a powerful way to grow your list, sell more and make your offers. Webinars also convert to sales better than a sales page alone.

If you're read this far, I have some questions for you:

Why aren't you using webinars to explode your business?

Are you worried that no one will show up?

What if you build your webinar and spend time and effort and no one shows up? It could happen, but not if you know the specific strategies on how to FILL up your webinar with your perfect, ideal potential customers.

Do you feel like an impostor?

Do you have a little voice that says, "Who am I to be hosting a webinar?"

You might get a little nervous, but knowing how to activate the Power Position, your expertise can shine and you can deliver tremendous value.

Are you scared because you don't know how to sell?

Are you afraid that things will go haywire when you start to pitch? Hey, you are NOT alone. You're great at teaching your irresistible, valuable content you to your audience. What you need are some solid strategies that allow you to smoothly move into the selling portion of your webinar with ease.

Good News!!! For every fear you have, there are precise strategies you can use to overcome them. The number #1 regret of successful webinar presenters is that they did not start sooner.

You CAN create webinars that will explode your business. Now's the time to create and deliver your first totally profitable webinar. Start with The Power of Webinars training program.

COACHING: Sherrie Rose, Webinar Coach

Go to: http://WebinarCoach.com

If you want to work with the #1 Rated Webinar Coach, then Sherrie Rose is ready to help you. Watch the short video and then go to schedule a call on the website and share your details. These are paid sessions so be prepared with your PayPal or credit card.

Ian Brodie, Marketing Speaker & Author of #1 Amazon Bestseller Email Persuasion, says:

I've done well over 100 webinars, yet Sherrie's coaching had a huge impact and resulted in a much more successful webinar.

Here's why Sherrie's such a good webinar coach:

1) She knows what works. She's worked with some of the best webinar marketers in the world and has a "kitbag" of techniques that will boost your webinar attendance, engagement and sales whether you're a beginner or an advanced webinar presenter.

2) She's a joy to work with. Prepping and delivering a big webinar is a high stress environment with tough timescales. Sherrie gets you through it and boosts your webinar with finesse. She knows when to push and when to support so that you get the very best results.

If you want better results from your webinars, I'd call Sherrie.

Jayne Warrilow, Specialist in Developing Leaders and Businesses that inspire the human spirit and Executive Coach, says:

"I recently worked with Sherrie to help me improve my webinar presentation for a global coaching audience. Although I consider myself experienced at running webinars, Sherrie's advice was exceptional. She completely transformed my slide deck to increase engagement and focus participant attention. What can I say? I received rave reviews and I give her my highest recommendation. She is a true expert in the field with deep content and she holds the key to what will work for your audience.

If you are thinking of working with Sherrie, just do it – you'll be thrilled!"

Suzi Pomerantz, #1 Bestselling Author, says:

"Sherrie worked with us to enhance our webinar in preparation for a large program launch. There is a fine art and a specific science to designing webinars for a launch, and Sherrie brought a mastery of both. She very quickly understood our content and audience and was able to contribute valuable guidance, wisdom, and expertise in the many iterations of the evolution of our presentation. She knows her stuff and is able to surgically hone in on how to take your webinar from drab to fab! If you're designing a webinar presentation to both teach and enroll, definitely bring Sherrie on board. She gets results!"

Andrew Neitlich, Founder and Director of the leading executive, leadership, and business training organization for coaches, says:

"It is rare that you get to work with a world-class expert or the best in class in anything. Sherrie Rose happens to be that person when it comes to creating webinars that generate serious results. She worked with me to create a webinar for an audience of high-end professionals that resulted in a 30% conversion rate. More importantly, Sherrie guided me through the process to make sure that everything was right, including: marketing the webinar, staying in touch with participants beforehand with value-added content, tactics to maximize webinar attendance, follow up to a variety of categories of participants after the webinar, and the webinar presentation itself. She also coached me through multiple rehearsals of the webinar to make sure that it was crisp and effective before the live events, and she moderated the webinar in ways that increased conversion. She also has helped take the webinar and turn it into an evergreen marketing program. Put simply, if you seek an expert in webinars that convert, you will not find a better resource than Sherrie. She is professional, personable, and fun to work with -- and she is committed to client results. Hire her."

## PART V

The Webinar Way Resources

THE WEBINAR WAY RESOURCES

Expert Interviews on The Webinar Way

Over 30 All-Star Interviews with Webinar Masters:

http://thewebinarway.com/allstar

Special Bonuses

The Webinar Way Profit Calculator

Sign up here: http://thewebinarway.com/

Persuasion Map: http://thewebinarway.com/2maps

RESOURCE LIST:

The Webinar Way Resources

The webinar resources are in a free, private members area. You will need this username and password to log in:

http://thewebinarway.com/resources

Username:	There are no spaces in the
WebinarWayMember	username. Both the
Password:	username and password
Wway$7P$	are CASE sensitive.

Here is a selection of just some of the webinar resources available to you:

- FAQS
- Hardware Recommendations
- Webinar Platforms
- Checklists, Worksheets
- Maps, Process Charts, Funnels
- Webinar Examples

The world of webinar software, platforms, and registration page builders is constantly improving. We attempt to keep these resources up-to-date.

HOT TRAINING: THE POWER OF WEBINARS

Sherrie Rose has created The Power of Webinars training system, which is a turn-key approach, completely systematized, and ready to go so you can get up and running fast! It is based on *The 7 Pillars of The Webinar Way.*

What you'll discover in our training are the "Essential" Webinar tactics, strategies, and core dynamics that are the **Keys to Wealth in Webinars.** Webinars put you in the Power Position to become the undisputed leader in your field and the obvious choice for your market.

The Power of Webinars is designed for you to learn how to build a webinar that converts like crazy, how to create an optimized webinar sequence, define your webinar marketing campaign, and plan a funnel with pre-webinar steps to create the DESIRE that ensures your participants show up. And we'll get you through any of your technical concerns.

Here's what's included in the training for **The Power of Webinars**:

- 9 Training Modules based on the 7 Pillars
- A Complete Step-by-Step Program
- Individual Lessons, Videos, Notes
- Customizable Slide Deck Template
- The Coveted "Cheat Sheets"
- Personal Support & Service
- Private Facebook Community
- Guest Experts Insights
- On-Demand Access
- Online Office Hours
- Spotlight on Your Live Webinar

- Amazing Valuable BONUS content
- Advanced 1-to-1 Coaching Calls
- Advanced Individual Practice Run
- Advanced Webinar Critique

Here's What You'll Create and Develop when you implement **The Power of Webinars**:

- A Webinar that Participants Love + Buy
- "Essential" Tactics, Strategies, Core Dynamics
- Fine Tune Your WAMO Formula
- Technology with you in Control
- Your Powerhouse Webinar Personality
- Compelling Marketing Plan Options
- Plan M.A.P. and a Funnel with Pre-webinar steps
- An Optimized Campaign Sequence
- Lead Magnet Review for Getting Attendees
- Webinar Registration Opt-In + Thank You Page
- An Exciting, Remarkable Slide Deck
- A Presentation that Teaches, Sells and Delivers
- An Ideal Audience Experience that Converts
- Invisible Persuasion With Continuous Benefits
- Successful Figures on Webinar Profit Calculator

The Power of Webinars training program guides you to BUILD A LUCRATIVE WEBINAR (or webinar series) by implementing real-world, tangible, step-by-step instructions to attract your perfect, ideal clients (even if you're getting started). Our goal is to quickly make your webinar profitable and for you to become a Webinar Powerhouse!

Go to: http://PowerofWebinars.com

ABOUT SHERRIE ROSE

Sherrie Rose spiraled into digital product and membership site creation after her first interview with the $10 Million Dollar man in 2009. As a *Relationship Investor* she blends marketing and her "Relationship Riches" philosophy with webinars.

Contact Sherrie for your webinar strategy session in preparation for your very first pilot webinar, or learn how to uncover more profits from an existing webinar.

- http://webinarcoach.com
- http://powerofwebinars.com
- http://twitter.com/sherrierose
- http://www.sherrierose.me
- https://www.facebook.com/asksherrierose
- https://www.facebook.com/sherrierose
- https://www.linkedin.com/in/sherrierose/

ABOUT THE WEBINAR WAY

"The Webinar Way is the #1 Way to reach global audiences and the #1 most effective sales tool using the Internet today."

Website: http://thewebinarway.com

Master Every *Serious* Entrepreneur's Favorite Wealth Builder: WEBINARS

- **Facebook Group**: https://www.facebook.com/groups/marketyourwebinars/
- **Facebook 1**: http://facebook.com/webinarway
- **Facebook 2**: http://facebook.com/webinarcoach
- **Facebook 3** http://facebook.com/powerofwebinars
- **Twitter:** http://twitter.com/thewebinarway @thewebinarway
- **Pinterest:** http://pinterest.com/thewebinarway/the-webinar-way/
- **Google+ Community** http://marketyourwebinars.com

POWER OF WEBINARS

Harness the full POWER of WEBINARS… and Become a Webinar Powerhouse!

- Get the Training Program here: http://PowerofWebinars.com/

Figure 10

FREE GIFT

Just in case you missed it earlier, you are eligible to receive a Free Webinar Strategy Session with Sherrie Rose

Go to: http://thewebinarway.com/claimit

Figure 11

Made in the USA
San Bernardino, CA
18 July 2018